Nehemiah Adams

A Voyage Around the World

Vol. 1

Nehemiah Adams

A Voyage Around the World
Vol. 1

ISBN/EAN: 9783337427726

Printed in Europe, USA, Canada, Australia, Japan

Cover: Foto ©Andreas Hilbeck / pixelio.de

More available books at **www.hansebooks.com**

A Voyage Around the World.

BY
N. ADAMS, D. D.

BOSTON:
PUBLISHED BY HENRY HOYT,
NO. 9 CORNHILL.

A VOYAGE ROUND THE WORLD.

CONTENTS.

I.
OUTWARD BOUND 9–36

II.
CAPE HORN 37–49

III.
CALIFORNIA. — THE SANDWICH ISLANDS. — HONG KONG . . 50–62

IV.
CANTON. — SHANGHAI. — SINGAPORE. — MACAO 63–112

V.
MANILA. — HOMEWARD BOUND 113–152

A Voyage Round the World

A VOYAGE AROUND THE WORLD.

I.

OUTWARD BOUND.

He travels, and I too: I tread his deck,
Ascend his topmast· through his peering eyes
Discover countries; with a kindred heart
Suffer his woes, and share in his escapes;
While Fancy, like the finger of a clock,
Runs the great circuit, and is still at home.
COWPER.

THERE are so many running to and fro, and knowledge is thereby so increased, that I doubted, at first, if my friends did well to ask me to write for publication an account of my voyage. But I considered that impressions made on every new observer add something to the already large information of intelligent readers, besides reviving agreeable recollections. The thought that I may suggest to some friend in need of long rest one means of finding it, or encourage him to adopt it, leads me to give, as requested, the following narrative.

The writer, having been ill in the early part of 1869, was advised by physicians and friends to try the effect of foreign travel; but in what direction it was difficult to decide. With every suggestion of experienced friends, there would arise some association of fatigue in sight-seeing, of monotony in resting long in one place. Pleasant as it would be to nestle in some quiet nook in Switzerland, or take up an abode in one of the Channel Islands, — Alderney, for example, where there would be much to gratify curiosity, and where the distance from the centres of information would not be great, — the thought of being confined to one place, or even district of country, or of being tempted to visit interesting scenes, and especially to make the acquaintance of interesting men, awakened such anticipations of labor as to forbid any hope of restoration from that source.

A son of the writer was compelled in youth by ill-health to leave his studies, and go to sea. In the fall of 1869 he received command of a commodious ship, the "Golden Fleece," which sailed in October of that year for San Francisco, Hong Kong, and Manila. By the kindness of Messrs. William F. Weld & Co., the writer and two members of his family accompanied him as passengers.

Many were the questions to which these passengers required answers previous to their embarkation on so long a voyage. The gale of September, 1869, which levelled our Boston Coliseum, and damaged so many steeples, and made such havoc among poplars, and other trees whose roots run near the surface, led to the inquiry, What were the ordinary chances of such gales at sea? This question was answered by producing the log-book of a recent voyage from Mexico, in which it appeared that the weather, day after day, was so free from any cause for fear, that the impression was allowed to gain strength that storms were an exception in sea-faring life. As to the gale just mentioned, it seemed safer to be at sea at such a time, with sea-room, than under roofs and chimneys, or in streets.

In two days after leaving New York we were in the Gulf Stream. We sailed through leagues of herbage which was borne from the shores by the Stream, and, like us, was going to sea. The ship rolled; and soon the wind freshened, and we were in a gale. We had our first sight of " mountain waves," so called; but they needed some imagination and a little fear to make them mountainous. They were enough, however, to make us uncomfortable. The gale lasted two days. We took the impression that such was to be the ordinary experience in the voyage, — discomfort and tediousness. But we were happy to find that it was not so; for, during the whole voyage, there were very few such experiences, — so infrequent, indeed, as to excite surprise when they came. The morning after the gale the weather was fine. Going on deck, we found we had exchanged the sharp air of the latter part of October in New England for the temperature of the early part of June.

Soon we were in the Tropic of Cancer. It seemed like a new world. Never before had we looked upon such a sky. There was no stratification in the clouds, and nothing of the cumulus formation; but the surface of the sky was composed of innumerable fleecy things moving in the gentlest manner, as though they feared to disturb slumber. The gentle motion was just the thing to induce sleep. As we thought of the turbulent state of the elements the day before, the sky now looked like an army which had been dismissed. It seemed as though there was not wind enough to form a large cloud. The hammock was made fast, one end of it to an iron belaying-pin in the saddle of the mizzenmast, in the shade of the spanker, and the other end to the rail. A hammock meets you at every point with the needed support. It brought strange sensations of rest to lie and listen to the plashing of the water against the sides of the ship. The measured roll of the vessel now was pleasurable. There was an easy swing to the hammock, as though a considerate hand were keeping it moving. How much better this rest and peace than travelling in Switzerland, or being pent up in the Azores, or wandering through Italy, if one needs rest and at the same time change of place! To an overworked brain here is seclusion indeed. There is here no post-office, with its delivery five times a day, so welcome on shore; no newspapers; no door-bell; no agents soliciting attention to new works, and begging you to put your name down and accept a copy, as though you had subscribed; no succession of engagements;

"No cares to break the long repose;"

no crowd of passengers, nor daily calculation

as to the day of arrival; nor jar of machinery, as in a steamboat, making you feel, day and night, that somebody is laboriously at work; and, to crown all, seemingly no end to your vacation.

But those clouds in the tropics! You had thought, perhaps, heretofore, that only at night the heavens declare the glory of God. Perhaps you find that the book which you brought on deck to read, but which you have no desire to open, may have in it a fly-leaf, on which, as you lie in the hammock, with one knee raised for a writing-table, you may indite these dreamy lines: —

THE CLOUDS IN THE TROPICS.

Did we not think o'er ocean's restless plain
To see embattled hosts, and feel the affray?
But lo! a truce is here, and gala-day;
Nor lines of march, nor rank and file remain.
The fleecy clouds move o'er the tranquil plain,
And fling their trade-wind signals to the breeze,
To Capricorn from Cancer, realm of peace!
They seek no martial order to regain,
But take some fancied likeness, one by one,

> Or shape themselves in wizard groups of things;
> No haste, nor deep designs, no jostling crowds.
> The hosts are going home, their service done.
> What sense of power the wide-spread quiet brings!
> In calms or storms "His strength is in the clouds."

The meteorology in the latter part of the Book of Job stood in no need of modern science to captivate the hearts of the worshippers of the true God. "Dost thou know the balancings of the clouds, the wondrous works of Him which is perfect in knowledge?"

The charm of sea-life in a sailing-vessel I found to be constant occupation of the mind without wearying it. At first it seemed a duty to read the periodicals which we brought with us, the new books reserved for the voyage, the choice articles in the quarterlies which had been commended to us. But for these we found no time. What charm could there be in Dante when a school of porpoises was in sight, each of them leaping out of water just for the pleasure of the dive back? If the mate called down the companion-way, "A sail on the lee-bow!" the paper-folder must keep the place in the uncut volume till you know all about her. It would be tedious waiting at a corner of a street ten minutes for a horse-car; but it was pleasant to wait an hour and forty minutes to come up with the stranger ahead, gaining upon her all the time, meanwhile watching the flying-fish which the ship started on the wing, or going forward into the bows and looking over to see the ship dash through the waves, with "a bone in her mouth," till suddenly the main topgallant-sail splits, and so fulfils the expectation expressed for the last five days that it could not long survive; and now, as it is the change of watch, and all hands are on deck, what could be more interesting than to see twenty-eight of them take in the old sail and bend the new one, then line the side of the ship with their curious faces to inspect the bark which we have now overtaken. She is the "Doon of

Ayr," one hundred and six days from Japan for New York, and, as she was tacking, we came so near that one might throw a biscuit on board. The captains of the bark and the ship had time for a few words of inquiry and information; then the two wanderers on the deep parted company, and watched each other for half an hour, and sighted each other, no doubt, occasionally, for an hour and a half, till each became to the other a speck. You have long ago forgotten your book, your journal, and magazine. This event and its many interludes are more interesting to you than a battle in Lord Derby's Homer; it is practical life; you begin to feel that every thing which you enjoy will be without the intrusion of periodical engagements, and you feel surprised that no such engagements now demand your thoughts.

Among the incidents at sea which give a charm to life, one is Speaking a vessel. This is a metaphorical expression, retained from the former days before signals were used in conversation, and when vessels had to come near enough to each other for the speaking to act its part. We had been out five or six days, when a sail was descried on the starboard bow. It proved to be a bark; and we were as glad to see her as though we had met an old friend in a foreign land. The bark soon hoisted her ensign, which was the same as raising your hat in passing. We hoisted ours, which was a signal of recognition. The bark ran up four flags, which we recognized by the spyglass as 6 9 5 7, showing her number in the book to be 6957. Turning to it, we read "Sachem." We ran up 4 5 9 1, our number in the book. The bark displayed 5 6 2 8, which we found to be "Salem." We showed 4 7 8 2, — "New York." The bark gave 6 8 7 4, — "Zanzibar." We returned 2 1 8 0, — "California." The bark showed 6, — "six days out." We did the same. The bark showed numeral pendant 54, meaning "longitude," and with it 54° 38'. We replied with 54° 30', — our calculation.

The bark then dipped her ensign, hauling it down half-way, then raising it again. This was done three times. We did the same, which was equivalent to "good-bye" on either side, and lifting the hat; we added 6 3 8 9, meaning, "Wish you a pleasant voyage." The answer was, 5 7 8 3, "Many thanks."

These courtesies at sea are pleasant. Coming up with the vessel, or she and you drawing near in passing, reading the numbers by the spyglass, and arranging all the signals, is an agreeable occupation for the larger part of two hours, including the departure of the vessels from each other, as though friends were parting, leaving the ocean more a solitude than before.

Meeting vessels, or passing them at a distance, exchanging signals, making out their numbers, bring remote parts of the earth suddenly to mind. Thus new trains of thought succeed each other entirely disconnected. I always enjoyed exercise on horseback for one principal reason,— that on horseback you cannot long pursue one train of thought. Your conjunctions are disjunctive. If you purpose to make out your evening lecture on horseback, your attention is so frequently taken by something in the road, or by the action of the horse, that you probably come home without any connected plan. So at sea. The occasional sight of a sail is an illustration of the charm of sea-life as having complete possession of your thoughts without leaving you long at liberty to pore over a subject. If you meet a Norwegian bark, and the captain tells you he is twenty-four days from Buenos Ayres, there is Norway and Buenos Ayres for your meditation, and perhaps for your statistical or geographical inquiry. If the "Queen of the Pacific," eighty-seven days from Macao for London, comes in sight, there is another chapter in the world's great miscellany. That sail yonder proves to be the "Hungarian," of Saguenay, twenty-one days out, bound to Melbourne, with lumber. You have another illustration of commerce binding together the ends of the earth. You soon excuse those friends of yours at home who commiserated you on the prospect of a long, monotonous sea-voyage. Where is the monotony? Not in the ship's clock, which enumerates every hour and half hour by a system of horology altogether different from shore time-pieces; not in the boatswain's "Pumpship" at evening, when twelve or fifteen men entertain you with a song. Every tune at the pumps must have a chorus. The sentiment in the song is the least important feature of it, — the celebration of some portion of the earth or seas, other than here and now: "I wish I was in Mobile Bay," "I'm bound for the Rio Grande," with the astounding chorus from twenty-eight men, part of whom the fine moonlight and the song tempt from their bunks, is an antidote to monotony.

The sailors were a merry set. Though only half of the crew — that is, one watch — were required each night at the pumps, all hands at first generally turned out because it was the time for a song. It was a nightly pleasure to be on the upper deck when the pumps were manned, and to hear twenty men sing. When making sail after a gale, the crew are ready for the loudest singing, unless it be at the pumps. For example, when hauling on the topsail halyards, they may have this song, the shanty man, as they call him, solo singer, beginning with a wailing strain:

  Solo: O poor Reuben Ranzo!   (twice.)
  Chorus: Ranzo, boys, Ranzo!
  Solo: Ranzo was no sailor!   "
  Chorus: Ranzo, boys, Ranzo!
  Solo: He shipped on board a whaler! "
  Chorus: Ranzo, boys, Ranzo!
  Solo: The captain was a bad man! "
  Chorus: Ranzo, boys, Ranzo!
  Solo: He put him in the rigging!   "
  Chorus: Ranzo, boys, Ranzo!
  Solo: He gave him six-and-thirty — "

by which time the topsail is mast-headed, and the mate cries, "Belay!"

When the mainsail is to be set, and they are hauling down the main tack, this, perhaps, is the song:—

Solo: " 'Way! haul away! my ro-sey;
Chorus: 'Way! haul away! haul away! JOE!"

the long pull, the strong pull, the pull altogether being given at the word " Joe ; " then no more pulling till the same word recurs.

When hauling on the main sheet, this is often the song, sung responsively:—

Shanty man: "Haul the bowline; Kitty is my darling.
Crew: Haul the bowline, the bowline *haul!*"

That no one may think of me above that which he seeth me to be, or that he heareth of me, let me say that I find, on inquiry, that the "main tack" is the *line* which hauls down that corner of the main sail which is toward the wind; called, therefore, the "weather clew." The "main *sheet*" hauls the other corner of the main sail; called, therefore, "the lee clew." Why a rope should be called a sheet is a piece of nautical metonymy which it would be difficult to explain. "Larboard" and "starboard" were formerly used to designate respectively the left and the right side of the ship, standing aft and looking forward; but the two words, so much alike, were not always readily apprehended, and so were changed to "port and starboard." Why the word "port" is used, does not appear; nor can any one tell why "Reuben Ranzo" is associated with one of the long pulls; if there be any philosophy in it, or historic association, it is as deep as the sea, or hopelessly lost.

After singing at the pumps, in good weather, when there was not much work, the men would have some amusement. Sometimes it was "Hunt the Slipper." Then, again, two men sat down opposite each other, their hands and feet tied, and a capstan bar was run through each of the two men's arms, behind him. The two would push each other with their feet till one would lose his balance, and fall over; then, being helpless, he was at the mercy of his comrade's feet till he begged for quarter. These games were interspersed with declamations. We had some of Macaulay's "Lays of Ancient Rome," "Spartacus," "My name is Norval." The merry laugh and the clapping of hands at the declaimers, and, now and then, the youthful voice of a boy reciting his piece from Henry Clay, or a story from the "Reader," beguiled many an evening in the tropics.

On crossing the line, one evening when we were on the upper deck, we were startled by a voice on the lower deck, "What ship's that?" The captain replied. The voice answered, "I shall call upon you to-morrow; I have an engagement this evening." At 2, P.M., the next day, being Saturday, we were summoned on deck by one of the sailors, who announced that Neptune was coming on board. All at once we saw a grotesque figure swinging in the air over the water, half-way up to the main topgallant, — the sailors pulling him in. He came on board, wet from his waist; and there came also over the sides a female figure and a young man. They came to the front cabin door, and saluted the captain, who stood ready to receive them. Neptune had on spectacles made of a tin can, epaulets of the same, buskins made of duck, long hair of rope-yarns, a duck tunic, and a girdle of twisted ropes. Mrs. Neptune had on a long duck mantle, her face blackened with burnt cork, and a large fan made of wood, and covered with sail-cloth; she used it gracefully. The son bore his father's trident, which was a four-pronged iron, called "the grains," used for spearing sharks. He, also, was fantastically dressed. They made obeisance to the captain, who welcomed them on board in a short speech. They then repaired to a booth fitted up as a sort of marquee, flung up the sides, and called a young man from the crew. They asked him if he ever crossed the line before; then set him in a barrel, with his feet out, inquired his name, where from and whither bound; and, as he opened his mouth to answer, inserted the paint-brush, filled with soap and lime, with which the son was lathering him, who then produced an old saw, fixed in a piece of wood for a sheath and handle, and shaved him. Neptune then ordered him to be washed; when four men took him and dipped him into a barrel of water. This they did to three young men. They then came up to our deck and saluted us. The captain informed them that we were all liege subjects of Neptune, and needed not to be sworn. They then wished us a pleasant voyage, — Mrs. N. taking her husband's arm, fanning herself gracefully, — and they withdrew. While it was a successful masquerade, well sustained in all the parts, — the boys consenting to be hazed, conscious that they were contributing something to the dramatic poetry of sea-life, — it was easy to see that it was capable of abuse. The officers saw that they should be careful how they allowed this liberty. To an invalid at sea these things are medicine; and, as I am writing in the interest of some who may betake themselves for the first time to sea in a sailing-ship for health, I would say that they must wait till they are in circumstances to find how "dulce est desipere in loco,"—how pleasant it is at sea to be even gamesome upon occasions.

One day, as I lay in the hammock, I found myself in a revery; my eye being fixed on a bright, new rope which appeared among the running rigging. I mention it as an illustration of the frames of mind which steal upon an invalid passenger, especially in a sailing-ship, because undisturbed there by a crowd, or by the noise of steam and its machinery. Would any one think that a single halyard among five or six others could bring to mind Burke's treatise on the "Sublime and Beautiful"? But it was even so. I found my eye going up the new rope in admiration at the perfect regularity in the twist of the strands. An artist cannot always combine the hempen yarns with the exactness which the ropemaker's wheel gives them. My eye went from the new rope to the old ones; all had the same perfect twist throughout the ship. The ropes, from belaying-pin to truck, the signal halyard and the hawser, seemed instinct with "the beauty of fitness," to borrow a term from the above-mentioned writer, — a common window-sash, with its parallelograms of panes, serving that great genius for an illustration.

> "Thus pleasure is spread through the earth
> In stray gifts, to be claimed by whoever shall find.
> Thus a rich loving-kindness, redundantly kind,
> Moves all nature to gladness and mirth." *

I cannot forget the simple pleasure which this meditation on a rope gave me, carrying me back to youthful days in my native place, and to the ropewalks there, the swift spindles, the horse in the cellar turning the wheel, the spinners, each with a bunch of hemp around him hitching it to the spindle, then

---

* Wordsworth. Poems of the Fancy, Stray Pleasures.

walking backwards, paying out the hemp through his hands with judicious care, the rope all the time growing lengthwise, down the walk. It used to be a wonder to me how the horse in the cellar, going about on the tan, could twist the twine at the end of the bridge as accurately as it was twisted at the spindle. Unconscious influence, remote causation, continents, oceans, years, intervening between the agent and the effect of his example and words, were illustrated by the horse in the ropewalk; and the revery would have been protracted, had not a vessel ahead caught my eye. Coming to my senses, I thought of Dean Swift's satire on Robert Boyle's pious and sentimental writings, which the Dean had to read in the hearing of Lady Berkeley, whose simplicity and enthusiasm he was pleased to ridicule, in revenge for the task imposed on him, under the guise of mimicking Mr. Boyle, in the famous verses, "Meditations on a Broomstick."

But few things have so pleasing an effect

in solving the kinks in one's brain as to lie in a hammock on deck at sea, far away from care, and let the fancy, like the poet's river, "wander at its own sweet will." This wandering would have continued, had I not been startled by descrying as aforesaid a vessel ahead, hove to, directly across our course, under short sail, her jib-boom gone, all looking as if she was in distress and trying to intercept us for relief. We began to consider how many we could accommodate in case she proved to be in a sinking condition; how our provisions would hold out; and other prudential questionings; which were soon dissipated by finding that she was a whaler with a whale alongside, a man standing on him cutting in, and the rest of the crew, some of them, hoisting up the pieces, and others trying them out. This episode in practical life contrasted well with the revery with which the forenoon begun, making with it a good illustration of the variety in sea-life.

It had rained in torrents one night, and it

kept on till nine o'clock the next day. The sailors stopped the lee scuppers, and soon the deck had eighteen inches of water on the lee side. The ducks were released, and thought their paradise regained. The sailors could not resist the opportunity to do a little washing; so flannel shirts and other articles of apparel came forth into the common tub, the lower deck; being trampled on by bare feet instead of the more laborious process of the washing-board. The sturdy limbs, bared up to the knees showed fine sets of muscles, enough to excite the admiration of an artist pursuing anatomical studies. After the sailors had finished, they turned their attention to the pigs, which were severally walked into the water on two legs by the men, when they were chased and knocked about and scrubbed, till, by their looks, they made you believe the saying of the market-men, that ship-fed pork has no superior. There was no monotony here.

But there was monotony soon in the doldrums. These are a region near the equator, between the north-east and south-east trades, where calms and rains abound, puffs of wind varying in direction every half-hour, trying to the sailors, disappointing the captain's hopes. He yearns for steam; even an old captain will resolve, for the hundredth time in his life, that he will never go to sea again; he jumps on his hat, and whistles for the wind. Then a breeze springs up, and he rubs his hands, and thinks that, after all, his ship is better than a steamer, till, in half an hour, she is almost motionless.

Then is the time for the sharks to appear. They are slow creatures, and cannot keep up with a good sailer; so in calms they come and lie alongside. The little pilot-fishes, the curious attendants of the shark, directing his attention to food, are with him. The grains are thrust at the shark; and, if they fasten in him, a bend of a rope around his tail brings him on board. Sailors have great spite against sharks; they may show tenderness to other creatures, but for sharks they have no mercy. They will use their sheath-knives about his nose, and disfigure him in all conceivable ways. Their theory is that a shark never dies till sunset. Sharks are hard to kill. You may cut off their heads and tails, and disembowel them, and even then the trunk will thrash the deck at so lively a rate that his executioners will have need to jump about for safety. In contrast with the shark, the dolphin seemed to me for beauty to verify all that poets have said of him. It is my belief that a dolphin's mouth is as perfect a curve as nature ever produces. His tints, when dying, are no fiction. Two sword-fish were caught one day, and the rapidity with which they were stripped of their flesh, and their back-bones hung up to dry, rivalled the skill and speed of young surgical practitioners.

We kept Thanksgiving, it having been appointed before we sailed, so that we knew the day. We dined at four, instead of our usual hour (half past twelve), and so we were at table part of the time with those at home. Our dinner was: — 1. Oyster soup; 2. Boiled salmon and scalloped oysters; 3. Roast fowl; 4. Huckleberry pudding; 5. Apple-pies of dried apple. Now, should any one envy us, or should his mouth water at such a bill of fare, let him know that oysters and salmon from tin cans are not the same as those fresh from Faneuil-Hall Market.

Before we approach and pass Cape Horn, it would be interesting, at least to the writer, if he should indulge in further minute descriptions of many other things in sea-life; but, interesting as these things may be to the writer, the reader may be supposed to know some things; and, intrepid as he may think himself, he must remember that there were brave men before Agamemnon.

II.

CAPE HORN.

> All places that the eye of Heaven visits
> Are to a wise man ports and happy havens.
> Teach thy necessity to reason thus:
> There is no virtue like necessity.
>
> SHAKSPEARE: *Richard II.*

AT six o'clock, A.M., Dec. 20, a man at the mast-head cried, "Land, ho!" We saw the highlands of Tierra del Fuego, about a hundred miles from Cape Horn. We lay on the water motionless. About a mile from us was a brig apparently bound the same way. The captain ordered a boat to be made ready; and the mate, one of the boatswains, and three sailors, rowed to her. She proved to be the brig "Hazard," Capt. Lewis, of Boston, belonging to Messrs. Baker and Morrill, eighty days from Malaga, bound to San Francisco, with raisins and lemons. The visitors received much information, and gave papers,— which, though fifty-seven days old, were gladly received,— some buckwheat, and other things, and received kind tokens in return. The swell would often hide the boat from the ship, and the ship from the boat, except the upper sails. In the afternoon the wind sprung up fair; soon we came close to, and the captains had conversation.

Tierra del Fuego lies south of Patagonia, separated by the Straits of Magellan. It has high hills, which, at a distance, look like domes. Many bays indent the coast, causing it to bend frequently. Between this district of country and Staten Land or Island, are the Straits of Le Maire, twelve miles broad. Entering the Straits with a fair wind and a strong current, on the morning of a bright, cool day, Dec. 21, we went at the rate of thirteen knots. We came alongside of a great patch of seaweed and kelp, on which were eleven large birds. We had tacked or had been becalmed for almost a week, losing nearly five days. We therefore enjoyed our speed the more. The hills were picturesque in the variety of their shapes; their jaggedness and grouping were beyond imagination. One cluster was surmounted by an enormous stone, fluted like a sea-shell, looking as if it were placed there for a memorial purpose.

There was another hill which terminated in the appearance of a man's head, the face upward, the features regular, and so much resembling one of the sailors that it received his name. Flocks of wild ducks, twenty or thirty in each, albatrosses, cape hens, cape pigeons, penguins or divers, were abundant. These penguins float with only the head above water, and dive often; they all made the scene most lively. We sat or stood three or four hours enjoying the wild enchantment. It was worth to any one a voyage from New York. We saw no trace of an inhabitant. They are said to be of large stature, almost naked, their skin and flesh toughened by the climate. They do no tillage, but live on shell-fish and game. I shall always remember this region for its wild beauty and seemingly intense barrenness.

We came up with a New-Bedford whaler; the name "Selah" was on her quarter, whale-boats over her side, and men at the masthead, looking for whales or seals. We also descried a large ship ahead of us which we overtook. She proved to be the "Cambrian," Liverpool, seventy days out. We enjoyed the sight of her, an iron vessel, with wire rigging, neat and handsome.

At length we saw Cape Horn Island, the object of our desire, and at 7, P.M., were abreast of it. Some high rocks stood about like sentinels. We were within a mile of the Cape.

Cape Horn Island is the southernmost extremity of Tierra del Fuego, in south latitude 55° 58'. It is the southern termination of a group of rocky islands surmounted with a dome-like hill, out of which is a projection like a straight horn. But Schouten, the Dutch discoverer, is said to have named Cape Horn from *Hoorn*, in the Netherlands, his native place. The whole hill is a bare rock; indeed, how could any thing, even the lowest forms of vegetable life, find root on a place smitten as this is by the waves? Only the lichens, stealing with seeming compassion over every form in nature doomed to barrenness, succeed in holding on to these rocks. The hill is about eight hundred feet high, its base environed by low, black rocks, with not a sign even of marine vegetation. One line of these rocks looks like a fort, the seeming gateway, higher than the rest of the wall, being composed of perpendicular fragments. All along the base of the rough hill, low, irregular piles, like a growth of thorns and brambles around a bowlder in a field, constitute a fringe, as though Nature felt that the place needed some appropriate decoration; and what could be more so than that which she has here given? For a long space toward the termination of the Cape, sharp rocks stand up in groups, and some apart, making a gradual ending of the scene, all in agreement with the wildness which marks the region.

The sight of this spot, one landmark of our continent, can never fade from the memory of the beholder. Like many a remarkable object, it is of moderate size, its impressiveness being due, not to its bulk or height, but to its position. At first you are disappointed in not seeing at such a place something colossal; you would have it mountainous; at least, you would have thought that it would be columnar. Nothing of this; you have the disappointment which you feel on seeing for the first time a distinguished man, whom you find to be of low stature, whereas you would have had him of imposing appearance. But soon, however, you feel that you are at one of the ends of the earth. Here the Atlantic and Pacific Oceans begin, the great deep dividing itself into those two principal features of our globe. Any thing monumental, any thing statuesque, or even picturesque, here, you feel would be trifling. Like silence, more expressive at times than speech, the total absence of all display here is sublimity itself; you would not have it otherwise than an infinite solitude, unpretentious, without form, almost chaotic. Around this point it is as though there were a contest to which ocean each billow shall divide: here the winds and waters make incessant war; the sea always roars and the fulness thereof. The rocks which finally terminate the Cape stand apart, as you sometimes see corners of blocks of buildings where an extensive fire has raged, and the most of the walls have fallen in; but here and there a shoulder of a wall overhangs the ruins.

We stood together as we passed the last landmarks, and sang,

"Praise God, from whom all blessings flow."

It had been a day, from beginning to end, of constant pleasure, from the moment that we entered the Straits of Le Maire. We had accomplished one great design in our voyage. Would that the pleasant theory that musical sounds leave their vibrations in the air might have reality given to it, and praise to God break forth from all of every language who navigate the Cape!

We had reason to feel that we were not a great way from circumpolar regions; for at a quarter before eleven, the night previous, there were lingering streaks of pink light in the west. We never before read out of doors so late in the evening as we did that 21st of December on deck.

We had been steering south, going five degrees below the Cape; now we needed to turn and go northward; but the fierce winds made no account of our plan. You may be several weeks trying in vain, as a ship belonging to our firm was, to double the Cape; but, by favoring winds, we were six days. Once only during this time had we a full view of the Horn; our captain had been here six times, and now, for the second time only, saw the Cape. Nothing lay between us and the Antarctic Circle and the South Pole. The waves were Cape-Horn swells, peculiar to that region. The sight of the ocean there was wild beyond description. Now and then the sun would come out, but his smile seemed sarcastic. Going on deck to view the tempest, you are made to feel, as the ship goes down into deep places, that you would be more surprised at her coming up than if she should disappear. It is a good time and place for faith. One of the Latin fathers said, " Qui discat orare, discat navigare;" Let him who would learn to pray go to sea. It is to be doubted whether there are many places on the globe where one feels the power of solitude precisely as here. In the depths of a wilderness, or among mountains, solitude is more like death; but here it seems to have consciousness; you are spell-bound by some awful power; there is an infinitude about these watery realms; it seems like being in eternity. In the ascent of Mont Blanc, while gazing from the Mer de Glace on those needles of granite, inaccessible except to the eagle, I once felt that nothing could exceed the sense of desolateness there inspired; but to be at the end of a continent, with two oceans separating and forming a wild raceway where they go asunder, all the winds and storms being summoned to witness the inauguration of two oceans, their frantic uproar seemingly designed for the great occasion, Patagonia and Tierra del Fuego with their stupendous solitudes listening to the clamor; and then the feeling that the next place recorded on the map is the Antarctic Circle, with its barriers of cold and ice, you are warranted in the conviction that you are as near the confines of unearthly dimensions as you can be on this planet. You think of home, and the thought of your separation from friends and country and your consignment to these awful wilds, gives you a feeling of littleness, of nothingness, seldom if ever experienced elsewhere. And here is the proud ship that stretched her length in the pier at New York so far as to hold her spar over the passing drays and reach almost to the opposite warerooms, now less than an egg-shell in these waters, — a tiny nautilus, a bubble, whose destruction any moment, unseen by any human eye, could not detain any of these proud waters to be so much as a mound over her grave.

One day, before we entered the Straits and reached Cape Horn, along the neighborhood of Patagonia, the sea was more than usually disturbed, a ground-swell succeeding a gale lifting the waves higher than we had seen them, so that the motion of the ship had no uniformity for any two consecutive moments during the larger part of the day, — a cold, cheerless day, the sun now and then shining faintly, the wind ahead, no chance for a nautical observation, everything to the last degree forlorn. A bird came, in all this turmoil, and lighted in the water near the ship, and swam about us. The sight suggested the following lines : —

THE CAPE-HORN ALBATROSS.

The ship lay tossing on the stormy ocean,
   A head wind challenging her right of way;
Sail after sail she furled; in exultation
   The waves accounted her their yielding prey.

On her lee beam the Patagonia coast line
   Keeps ambushed reefs to snare the drifting keel;
We fancied breakers in the dying sunshine,
   And questioned what the daybreak would reveal.

No cities, towns, nor quiet rural village
   Gladden the heart along this lonely way;
But cannibals may lurk with death and pillage
   For all whom winds and currents force astray.

The Falkland Isles, Tierra del Fuego,
   Straits of Le Maire, the near Antarctic Zone,
The stormy Horn, whose rocks the tempest echo,
   Can faith and courage there maintain their throne?

Watching the swell from out the cabin windows,
   The towering waves piled high and steep appear;
But what is riding on those mighty billows?
   An albatross. The sight allays my fear.

Her snow-white breast she settles on the water,
    Her dark wings fluttering while she trims her form,
Then calmly rides ; nor can the great waves daunt her,
    Nor will she heed the menace of the storm.

She spreads her wings, flies low across the vessel,
    She scans the wake, then sails around the bows,
Not moving either pinion ; much I marvel
    How like one flying in a dream she goes.

She craves the presence of no other sea-bird ;
    She revels in the power to go at will ;
The ocean solitudes, the wandering seaward,
    The distant sail, her daring spirit thrill.

Behold, this fowl hath neither barn nor storehouse ;
    An unseen Hand assists her search for food ;
Storms bring her up deep things of ocean's produce,
    Prized the more highly in the storm pursued.

With joy each day I'll take the wings of morning,
    Dwell in the utmost parts of this lone sea ;
E'en there thy hand shall lead me, still adoring,
    And thy right hand shall hold who trust in thee.

III.

CALIFORNIA, THE SANDWICH ISLANDS, HONG KONG.

> Long have they voyaged o'er the distant seas;
> And what a heart-delight they feel at last,
> So many toils, so many dangers past,
> To view the port desired, he only knows
> Who on the stormy deep for many a day
> Hath tossed, a weary of his ocean way,
> And watched, all anxious, every wind that blows.
>
> SOUTHEY.

ONE day, at sundown, the captain said, as he looked at his watch, "At five minutes past nine this evening we shall see Faralone Light." We had tacked several times that day; the current was strong, the wind had come round aft, so that only one course of sails drew; therefore, we paid little attention to the remark, supposing it to be a guess, or at least a hope, rather than a judgment.

At nine o'clock, a man was sent aloft to see if there was a light visible. At twenty minutes after nine he called out, "Light, ho! three points on the port bow." In five or ten minutes we saw it from the deck.

We felt that this part of the voyage was over. We had been round Cape Horn, we had sailed back to 37° N., and were now also far west of Boston.

It would be gratifying to indulge in full descriptions of San Francisco and the enjoyment derived from valued friends; but this is superfluous.

An earthquake, a few days after we were on shore, was the first experience I had ever had of that kind. Cape Horn did not shake after that manner. It seemed desirable to be at sea in order to be safe.

The view of the Pacific from the Cliff House seemed to me one of the finest sea-views from shore which I ever enjoyed.

I saw it stated in a San Francisco periodical that the coast-line of California, taking in its indentations and curves, is equal to a straight line drawn from San Francisco to Plymouth, Mass.

One day, in driving, we came to a hill, which, though it was as early as March 15, had begun to put forth verdure, and the hill was clothed with a combination of colors more numerous and brilliant than I ever saw in any part of our travels. I left this wonderful region with great love for it, and with deep impressions of the characters of the many new friends which I had found.

Proceeding to the Sandwich Islands at the request of our agents, to receive freight there for China, we sailed by the whole group, forever memorable in the history of modern Christianity. We anchored as advised by the pilot, but were too near the reef to feel safe should we have a gale. The wind was very strong; and, as we learned that there was no freight, we raised anchor and went on our way, we approving of the captain's judgment that any gratification we might have in viewing the scene of missionary success would hardly warrant the detention of the ship. We had kind messages from Dr. Judd, who offered to ask Capt. Truxton, of the United States vessel " Jamestown," to send his yawl for us if we would stay. H. M. Whitney, Esq., editor of " The Honolulu Commercial," politely sent us an invitation to his house during our visit, should we come ashore. But our captain judiciously decided to proceed on our voyage at once. We had enjoyed a fine view of the islands. Since leaving Tierra del Fuego, no such picture of desolation had presented itself as the approaches to Honolulu with its volcanic relics. Rev. Hiram Bingham and S. B. Dole, Esq., both sons of missionaries, came off to see us, and gave us valuable information. They confirmed previous accounts of the rapid decrease of the native population, who seem to have little vital force, but are suddenly overcome by sickness, and die after a very brief illness. The tolling of the bell day after day is a constant dirge over the wasting lives of these islanders. There is a disposition there to try a less obnoxious system of church ordinances, which will, no doubt, secure a hold for liturgical worship among many of the foreign residents and their offspring; and good feeling seems likely to prevail. If systems diverse from the views of those who have wrought such achievements in those islands seek a shelter there, and the birds of the air come and lodge in the branches of our great tree, may they be well-disposed birds, remembering who planted, who watered, while God gave the increase.

We took a supply of the largest and sweetest oranges and of the best bananas I ever saw. The attractive style in which "The Honolulu Advertiser" is arranged and printed, gave me favorable impressions of the state of the practical arts in Honolulu. In the fine moonlight night we sailed away from this most interesting group, for China. There is no part of the world which I have seen which I would sooner revisit, or where I should expect greater enjoyment, than the Sandwich Islands.

Of all the bright days which have gladdened our way, none have surpassed those which we spent in going from the Sandwich Islands to China. Existence was a charm in that beautiful climate, that trade-wind region. Thirty-three days of perfect weather, one succeeding another with seemingly new beauty, made us feel that we had left this world of storms. If I ever need an emblem of perfect peace, the voyage from the Sandwich Islands to China will be sure to revive in my memory.

With new sensations of interest we reached the China Sea. The Bashee group of islands marks one entrance to it from the Pacific. We passed close to the island of Belintang. Here I had a first imaginary glimpse of the heathen world in a singular spectacle, which I would have said was an illusion, had not all whom I asked to notice it agreed that it was a remarkable object.

About sixty feet from the island, in the water, stands a high rock, in the shape of a flattened ellipse, wholly isolated. Its base looks as though it were stuccoed with large sea-shells, the grooved side of each facing you. One-half of the elevation is shapeless, but the other half is as good an image of a monstrous idol god as can be found.

> " What seemed a head,
> The likeness of a kingly crown had on,"

or, perhaps, a mitre or a fillet. The eyes are like the eyes of a plaster bust, made by two protuberances of the rock, volcanic blisters; and over the whole figure seems to be thrown a rude drapery, which a little fancy converts into a robe. The whole effect is that of a huge idol god. There it stands at the gateway of the China Sea; and, if superstition had employed sculptors and architects to set up an image of Buddha there, no better result

THE BASHEE IMAGE.—page 57

could have been achieved. No hand, however, founded this on the seas and established it on the floods. There is a marine picturesqueness about the rock as a whole which is very fine. I am thus minute in the description, hoping that some who read these lines will, on seeing the Bashee image, make a more full description.

On the 13th of May we dropped anchor in Hong Kong Harbor. Five miles out, two pilots hailed us from opposite points, each in his rude sampan, their sails of matting and their oars combining to bring each first to the ship. The wind favored one, who came astern and caught a rope, which he nimbly climbed and came aboard. There was a woman with an oar sculling and steering, while her husband and one or two boys and girls managed the sails. On her back her infant was strapped, a boy sixteen months old, as we were informed. The little fellow had to endure all the motions of his mother at the oar, peeping over each of her shoulders by turns, and holding her neck with his hands. This, we found, is the common mode of life among infants here, children eight years old being harnessed to the employment of thus carrying about their infant brothers and sisters.

We found ourselves at once surrounded by vessels of all nations. More than two hundred were in port. We lived aboard ship, where we were cool; were visited by gentlemen and ladies, and by masters of vessels, whose ships we visited in return. The Chinese tradesmen came on board almost every day with their wares, the deck being covered with their manufactures of ivory and silver. This is an English colony, a free port. Among the people in the streets are Parsees from Persia, who deal in the productions of their country, and Sepoys from Hindostan. These latter are police-officers and soldiers, black as charcoal, tall, straight, well-proportioned men.

Hong Kong, or Sweet Waters, is an island. Some of its districts are Stanley, Pokfalum,

Aberdeen, Victoria, of which the latter is the principal, being the seat of government. Victoria Peak, overlooking the harbor and vicinity, is about eighteen hundred feet high; on it is a signal station, and the arrival of steamers and government vessels is made known by a field-piece at the summit. The winding ascent is extremely fine. This peak is ascended in sedan-chairs, each borne by four coolies. The ascent is made in one hour. The road winds continually, presenting fine views of the coast, the shipping in the harbor, and ranges of mountains, and groups of islands.

We went on shore to church, after our service with the sailors in the morning, and attended worship at Rev. Dr. Legge's chapel, known as "Union Church." It is a beautiful building, on an elevated spot, with foliage of the bamboo trees around it. Over the speaker a punka of blue silk was kept in motion by a coolie out of sight, making it comfortable for the preacher. Good Dr. Duff protested against punkas in the church as luxurious and worldly. After being in the East India climate a while, he said, "I must have a punka over me when I preach here." I preached for Dr. Legge the next Sabbath morning, and five or six other times, and went ashore again in the afternoon occasionally to the chapel, and once heard the Rev. Mr. Turner, a missionary sustained by a British society, preach to a congregation of Chinese. I was struck with their devout appearance in prayer. All was unintelligible till the doxology, in Old Hundred.

English schools for Chinese youth, maintained here by the government, one of them with over one hundred and fifty young men, taught by Mr. Stuart, I had the pleasure of visiting, and was interested to hear the native youths read well in English, with little Chinese accent.

We enjoyed living here among the ships under strange flags. The officers of several United States vessels were polite to us, and afforded us much pleasure by their intelligent society.

Rev. Dr. Legge, the eminent Chinese scholar, is engaged on his five or six large volumes of the Chinese classics. The Doctor is not impressed with the intellectual ability of Confucius nor of his followers. His translations are invaluable, as saving missionaries and other students of the Chinese much pains by placing Chinese literature before them in a digested form. One could not help regretting that this laborious scholar cannot have the advantage of an international copyright law to afford protection to his costly fruits of research. American authors suffer the same loss, however, as he, in seeing their valuable works appropriated by foreigners.

It was with a feeling of national pride that we saw the Pacific Mail Company's steamer "China," Capt. Doane, thirty days from San Francisco, come into the harbor promptly on the day she was due. She is a noble ship of four thousand tons. Capt. Doane came on board our ship, and invited us to inspect his vessel. It is one of the principal events of the month with Americans to have the Pacific Mail Steamer appear. All other steamers seem diminutive by the side of them. It seemed strange to find on board these vessels five or six live oxen and the appurtenances of a slaughter-house, — bestowed, however, out of sight.

We staid in Hong Kong six months waiting for hemp to fall in Manila. While the ship lay at anchor we enjoyed the privilege, by the favor of Messrs. Augustine Heard & Co., of visiting several places in China and the East Indies. Some account of a visit to Canton, Shanghai, Singapore, and Macao, and then of the ship's departure to Manila, and thence to New York, will have enabled the reader to belt the globe.

IV.

CANTON, SHANGHAI, SINGAPORE, MACAO.

> This is a traveller, sir; knows men and
> Manners, and has ploughed up the sea so far
> Till both the poles have knocked; has seen the sun
> Take coach, and can distinguish the color
> Of his horses and their kinds.
> — BEAUMONT AND FLETCHER'S "*Scornful Lady.*"

THE city of Canton is only eight hours by steamer from Hong Kong. Arriving in the Canton River, you find yourself in a floating population in boats, close together, as though ground rents were as dear as in Broadway. When you enter a boat for a passage up the river, you marvel that the boat can extricate itself from the snarl; but you are, in a few moments, on your way, meeting a seemingly endless throng of people, among whom you involuntarily close your eyes as if in anticipation of a crash. We were the guests of the Rev. Dr. Happer of the American Presbyterian Mission, who, on our arrival at Hong Kong, had kindly invited us. We were also entertained by the other members of the Mission, — Messrs. Noyes, Marcellus, and McChesney. We visited Dr. Ker's hospital. Over a hundred Chinese were sitting in a commodious room listening to a native evangelist, and going out by tens to receive medical treatment. This hospital was formerly sustained by the American Board of Foreign Missions, with Dr. Peter Parker for surgeon and physician.

Being introduced to Archdeacon Gray, he very kindly went with us two afternoons among the temples and many remarkable places. We saw the temple in which are five hundred bronzed images of gods or deified men, each in a posture, or holding an emblem, representing some action or attribute. We saw the water-clock, made by tubs of water placed one above another, each dripping into the one below it, and the lowest holding a graduated stick which rose through a hole in the lid, and as each hour-mark on the stick appears through the hole, a man goes up to the roof with a painted sign announcing to the people the time of day. This seems to be an heirloom from past ages, when the "Clepsydra" was in use, of which this is a specimen. Adherence to this useless thing is one illustration of the Chinese attachment to antiquity. As you go about the city, you see things which carry you back two thousand years, — oxen treading clay, men sifting wheat in sieves fastened on the ends of planks laid on rolling stones, and a man standing on each and keeping up a motion on the planks like "tilting," or "seesaw," — a laborious process of doing a simple thing. Then you see works of art surpassing modern western skill; as, for example, an elephant's tusk undergoing three years of carving; price, one hundred and fifty dollars. Then you visit an eating-house, which Archdeacon Gray begs you to endure, to know that some things related of the Chinese are not fictions. He goes to a man who is eating, and, courteously taking up his plate, says, "What is this?" The man laughs and tells him. He goes to another, and, taking his plate, says, "What is this?" The man cheerfully replies; but let it be untranslated. Around the room, on hooks, are evident signs that the men were truthful. You make swift retreat, but are constrained by your guide to look into an opium shop, where the customer, as he comes in, mounts a table, lies at full length, with his head on a wicker pillow hollowed in the middle to fit the neck, then is furnished with a pipe and lamp and box of opium, which he smokes till he is stupefied. Emerging from such scenes of degradation into the narrow street, ten feet wide, you may see a woman at a door with a child three years old, with whom she is playing "pease porridge hot," going through the motions as we learned them in childhood; and you wonder whether Mother Goose derived her knowledge from the disciples of Confucius, or whether she did actually live and die, as is now asserted, in Rowe Street, Boston. This Chinese woman and her child playing at " pease porridge hot," is one of those touches of nature which make " all the world akin." You next reach a place where intellectual competition throws some of our university intellectual feats into the shade. It is the Hall of Competitive Examination, of which there is one in each of the eighteen provincial cities of China. Though familiar by description, perhaps, to the reader, I venture to repeat that it is a large open ground, — the one in Canton measuring 689,250 square feet. On one hand, there are seventy-five lanes containing 4,767 cells; on the other, sixty-eight lanes with 3,886 cells, making a total of 8,653 cells. Once in three years, men of every age, from the youth to the aged, assemble to write prize essays for a literary degree. A candidate is fastened into each cell for three days and nights, with rice and water, planks being fixed in grooves in the sides of the cell serving for a sleeping place, and for a writing-table by day. The strictest search is made to see that no book or paper is secreted in any dress. The essays are received by three officers, who seal up the outside page of each essay, on which is written the name, age, residence, ancestors, &c., of the writer. They are passed to another officer, who sees that they are copied in red ink,— the object of the copying being that the original handwriting may not be recognized by the judges. Nearly two thousand writers are employed in copying. They have rooms fitted up for them in the "Hall of Perfect Honesty." The governor of the province is ex-officio chief superintendent. Imperial commissioners from Pekin assist in the examinations. They meet in the "Hall of Auspicious Stars." This hall is looked upon with feelings of awe mingled with hope. Success in these examinations is followed by fame, wealth, and honor; and failure, by years of toil and possibly of repeated disappointment. Messengers wait to carry the names of the successful candidates to every part of the province. The governor gives them a feast; after which they go in state dress to worship the tablets of their ancestors. Odes, as well as essays, are presented. The following are specimens of the themes at the last examination previous to 1870: —

"If the will be set on virtue, there will be no practice of wickedness."

"It is only the individual possessed of the most entire sincerity that can exist under heaven, who can adjust the great, invariable interests of mankind."

"There are ministers who seek the tranquillity of the state, and find their pleasure in securing that tranquillity."

What can be more abstruse? Few among us would attempt to be original on such themes.

This system of competitive literary examinations, here imperfectly described, has been maintained more than a thousand years. There are records proving this. On the first day, three essays and one piece of poetry are required; each essay must have seven hundred words, the poetry must consist of seven hundred and sixteen lines, with five words in each. The pieces required on the other two days vary from this. The successful competitors are immortalized in fame; their triumph goes down to posterity on the family tablets, is noted on their tombs, secures honor to their children.

Though I visited this "Hall" with Archdeacon Gray, and received minute information from him, I am since indebted for helps to my memory to a paper read before a literary society in Canton, by Dr. J. G. Ker.

One morning some of my party were standing by the window of a friend's house in Canton which overlooks the canal with its brown water and crowd of sampans. As they watched the different phases of domestic life in those habitations, one of the party, familiar with them, remarked that there was probably a wedding, or rather the festivities attendant upon a wedding, in one of the nearest sampans, as she had heard a young woman wailing the night before. She said it is a custom with Chinese brides to pass the night before their weddings in bewailing their future troubles; for, as they seldom see their intended masters before the wedding, there is great uncertainty in connection with their new mode of life; generally it is going from one form of servitude into one to which they had not grown accustomed. There seems to be no real wedding ceremony, but a feast and a sort of reception for three days. During that time the young couple perform some acts of devotion before the ancestral tablets. After that the bridegroom takes his partner to his father's boat, where she cooks the rice, scrubs, and helps row for the rest of her life.

The young ladies thought that they would

go to the reception. Accordingly, eight of them crowded into the sampan (being told that no cards were used) and sat in Turkish fashion on the nice floor. The bride came before them in a red dress, saluted them, then brought in a tray of square cakes, which had been made with peanut oil. She then gave them tea in small cups such as children play with. They considered that, as the tea was made with the foul water of the canal, occupied by a crowd of sampans, it could not be in the highest degree tasteful. As they went out, they were told that the adjoining boat was the home of the bridegroom's father, where the bride would the next day find her home. A roasted pig, with its garniture of herbs, was exposed on deck, but it did not awaken any desire.

We were greatly favored, through the influence of Archdeacon Gray, in having the rare privilege of being admitted to the bedchamber of "the god of Walled Cities." We climbed up antique, decayed stairs into a forlorn room, not so inviting as apartments in some barns at home. There was the huge god, six feet in height; his slippers were at the side of his bed; his garments were on pegs; the wash-stand was there, with its furniture, and the water was poured into the bowl ready for use. His Majesty was of wood fantastically painted. We were taken into his wife's apartment, which was the next room. There women resort to make petitions with vows, promising the goddess a new dress, for example, if their prayer is heard.

In several temples we saw men consulting the gods in some affairs of interest to them. Kneeling and touching the ground with the forehead nine times, they would then take a long box of sticks, each with a number inscribed on it, shake it till a stick fell out, which was then handed to the priest, who consulted a book, and told the petitioner the answer to his prayer.

We came in one temple to the " Chamber

of Horrors." There in ten cells were depicted the torments awaiting the wicked in the next world. In the tenth the victims were coming out in the shape of hideous wild animals, the blessed dead, on eminences around, looking down with various expressions on their faces. We came also to the " Temple of the Five Genii," — Fire, Earth, Water, Wood, and Metals. These Genii originally came to the city on five rams, which were turned to stone, for perpetuity, and remain there to this day, uncouth, almost shapeless blocks. A tower said to be six hundred years old stands in honor of them. The large bell covered with Chinese characters is doomed to silence ; for there is a tradition that if struck, some great misfortune would fall upon the city. A visitor inadvertently striking it would excite consternation among the people. During a siege of Canton a piece of the bell was knocked out of it by a cannon-ball.

While we were detained by rain in a temple, the Buddhist priests showed us much kindness, setting a table in the courtyard overlooking a sheet of water, and giving us clear tea in little cups, on trays having, each, compartments filled with dried fruits. It seemed strange to be " sitting at meat in an idol's temple." While we were there, the priests descried the sunshades which some of the party had brought with them. Their amusement was not exceeded by any pleasure manifested by children at the sight of new things. They opened them, they shut them, turned them over and over, held them over one another, explaining to each other their use ; and one man, pointing to one of our umbrellas, said, " That I can understand ; but is this really an umbrella ? "

As our party of four emerged from their chairs at each temple, crowds of a hundred or more would follow us to the gate, and wait there for us to re-appear. Mothers would lift little children to see the odd foreigners. Not one word, sign, or look of contempt or disrespect, however, did we witness during the four or five days that we spent in the city. The streets being, most of them, only eight or ten feet wide, the people were frequently stopped by our chairs, and had to stand sideways to let us pass, but never did they make us feel that we were intruders. About two months after this, the affair at Tientsin happened, and the people in many parts of the empire were excited to some degree against foreigners. Receiving an invitation to revisit Canton, I was strongly advised not to go, on the ground, that, while mercantile men, obviously on business, might visit the place in safety, the sight of a foreigner, led there by curiosity, might awaken suspicion and lead to violence.

Archdeacon Gray is well known to all who have visited Canton. He is in the prime of life, an accomplished gentleman, making you love him at once by his beautifully courteous manner, his fine intelligence. He gave me a cordial invitation to occupy his pulpit on sabbath morning; but there was to be a communion service at the Presbyterian Mission, with some additions to the church, and I declined. But he came in the intermission, and insisted on my preaching in the afternoon, which I did. His house and church are on a bend of the Canton River; and perhaps even our Hudson River does not anywhere present a finer view. His house is full of rare Chinese curiosities, which he is happy to show to visitors. I preached in the evening to the Presbyterian Mission, at the house of one of their number. This Mission is exerting a decided influence; its supporters may well be encouraged. I found a strong feeling among them in favor of sending out single ladies, in companies, to live together and to labor in conjunction with the Mission. There is a decided conviction in the Canton Mission that ladies, living together, and working under the direction of a mission, will be the most powerful of auxiliaries.

I spent four or five days at Shanghai, on

another excursion from Hong Kong. This I described in a letter to Bishop Eastburn, as several things which I saw there in connection with Episcopal friends made it agreeable to acquaint him with them. The letter was kindly published in "The Christian Witness" of this city, and copied by "the Boston Transcript." I take this opportunity to insert the most of that letter, from one of the papers above mentioned.

HONG KONG, CHINA, October 10, 1870.

MY DEAR BISHOP EASTBURN,— I shall not soon forget that the first letter which met my eye on reaching San Francisco, after a voyage of one hundred and eleven days, was in your handwriting. I have since then been so pleasantly reminded of you, through a good man's influence here in China, that I must tell you of it. Being on a visit to Shanghai, I was invited to attend worship in a Chinese chapel five miles from the city. We went through the fields in chairs borne by coolies, till we came to the village where trade was plying all its arts and handicraft its implements, unconscious of the sabbath. A small church-bell notified us that we were near the chapel; and soon we emerged from heathenish sounds and sights into a Christian temple, neat and orderly in all its appointments. There were about one hundred and fifty Chinese assembled for worship, which was conducted by a very good-looking Chinaman, tall, and of pleasing address. Though ignorant of every word he said, my attention was riveted by his agreeable action and manner, eminently becoming a preacher of the gospel, and, withal, truly eloquent, if his whole appearance and the attention of the people were true indications. I could see that the services were liturgical, from the responses, and from the Chinese books used by the people, the little girls around me keeping my attention directed to the place in the service; though very little good did this do me, except that it helped me to keep my book right side up. The service ended with singing, "There is a happy land," the tune so familiarly known in our sabbath schools. The preacher came to speak with me before service, with his welcome in very good English; and after service he came again and gave me much information. He has been rector there sixteen years, the chapel being built and he being sustained there by the munificence, said he, "of a Mr. William Appleton, of Boston." This made my heart leap for joy, to come so far into heathenism and find myself in a Christian temple erected and maintained by a fellow-citizen of Boston. Mr. Appleton I did not know personally, though I once received a very kind note from him with a pamphlet. But I had long cherished a sincere love for him from many impressions of his truly estimable character. I was led to think, What a memorial of Christian zeal has he built in this distant land! What pleasure it must afford his happy spirit in heaven to look down on this place of Christian worship in the depths of heathenism! What a noble use of wealth, blessing a multitude of people who but for him might have been left in heathenish ignorance! I told the preacher that I should report his chapel and his labors to Christian friends at home, and I mentioned your name in speaking of those who would be glad to hear of him. He desired me to give his respects to you; so it is my pleasure to send you the respectful and Christian salutation of the Reverend Wong Kwong Chi, of one of the villages of Shanghai.

As we came out of the chapel, our ears were saluted with some musical instruments from a house where people were making a tumult over a dead person. Little knew they of that "happy land, far, far away," which the people of Appleton Chapel had just been celebrating. I felt a desire to tell good men in Boston that there yet remaineth much land to be possessed here by Christian philanthropists; that they can readily find villages of sixty thousand waiting each for its chapel, to say nothing of cities with millions in them, where it would be easy to begin a work for the ransomed spirits of good men and women to review with pleasure in heaven. Truly enviable is that rich Christian who can employ wealth to do good for him when he is with Christ. The Appleton Chapel at Shanghai seemed to me a cup of cold water, the donor of which is not losing his reward.

From the steamboat-landing at Shanghai, looking across the river, you see a comely church of fair proportions, surrounded in part with banyan and bamboo trees, affording it a perpetually verdant appearance. It is a stone chapel for seamen, built through the efforts of A. A. Hayes, Jr., of the firm of Olyphant & Co., and son of Dr. A. A. Hayes, of Boston. It is under the care of the Rev. Mr. Syle, Presbyterian, a devoted and most useful man.. A large churchyard has there received the remains of seamen of all nations. It is within the same enclosure with the church, ornamented with plants and trees, and is nearly filled with the dead. It has been opened fourteen years, and there are fourteen hundred interments. The graves are in close and even rows, for economy of room, so that this large collection of the dead looks like a buried battalion who have lain down by platoons. The orderly disposal of them has a saddening influence. I never before felt that there is a natural appropriateness in having a burial-place, as Job says of the land of the departed, " a land without any order." We feel that promptitude and exactness are out of place at a funeral; but slowness and delay are congenial. Surely, these ranks of the dead will not rise by roll-call, though they lay down in such good order. They made me think of some lines of an uncle of Sir Walter Scott, a sea-captain, on a sunken man-of-war, all her crew on board: —

> " In death's dark road at anchor fast they stay,
> Till Heaven's loud signal shall in thunder roar;

> Then, starting up, all hands shall quick obey;
> Sheet home the topsail, and with speed unmoor."*

One of the most charming places in China, is Macao, three hours distant by steamer from Hong Kong, the people of which place resort to Macao in the hot season, as the fine sea-breezes there greatly mitigate the heat. The drives about the place, commanding in every direction an open sea-view, are beautiful. The old church of St. Paul, the most of which remains, though ruined by fire, is a fine specimen of architecture. The most notable thing in Macao is the grotto where Camöens, the Portuguese poet, died in banishment for publishing a satire on the viceroy. The wild botany of the place, and the geological upheavals which give clear signs of glacial action, are

---

* I may as well give here all the lines of the "old tar," relating to the shipwreck:—

> No more the geese shall cackle o'er the poop;
> No more the bagpipe through the orlop sound;
> No more the midshipmen, a jovial group,
> Shall toast the girls, and push the bottle round.
>
> In death's dark road at anchor fast they stay,
> Till Heaven's loud signal shall in thunder roar;
> Then, starting up, all hands shall quick obey;
> Sheet home the topsail, and with speed unmoor.

remarkable. Bowlders are piled up here in ways which show a hydrodynamic force beyond human skill. Near the grotto is a cemetery for foreigners; and, among the many sainted dead from missionary circles there entombed, the Christian traveller lingers with deep interest around the burial-place of Morrison.

One sabbath morning I went with a Christian friend through a wild district, in the neighborhood of a large city in China, to a mission station. The people were everywhere at work; nothing suggested the sabbath till we heard the little church-bell, whose notes were in pleasing contrast to the hum of business. We came to the mission compound, where two missionaries and their wives had their abode. The joy with which they welcomed us made us feel most deeply their isolation from Christian society. The sight of friends from America seemed to intensify their loneliness. Here were four beloved Christian people who were living in these wilds to teach these heathen tribes the knowledge of God and of his Son. On inquiring what encouragement they found in their work, we were told that two or three women had lately shown a disposition to hear religious conversation and listen to the Scriptures. Immediately we thought of four hundred millions in China and its dependencies, who were ignorant of the true God. Here were three native women who were persuaded to listen to religious reading. As we were preparing to leave, our missionary friends seemed to cling to us with strong affection. We were going back to America, leaving them in the solitudes of heathenism. They were far from unhappy, and their few tears were only the natural expression of awakened memories. One of the missionary brethren, showing us the way to the gate, passed with us through a room where we saw, among gardening tools, some sheets of paper lying loose. There were so many of them, looking alike, that they attracted our notice. We found that the specks on them were the eggs of silkworms. They were mere dots, as the reader familiar with the sight in books or nature, is aware. It occurred to me what a display of silk fabrics, with their rainbow colors, we had been looking upon! how many ships are freighted with them! how many millions of wealth they represent! what a world of thought and feeling is associated with them! On those pieces of paper were the beginnings of silk, — a word, taken in all its connections and associations, of mighty power. In those little specks one might fancy himself reading, "By whom shall Jacob arise? for he is small." We told our missionary brother, that, while he raised silkworms and saw their cocoons, he surely would never despise the day of small things, — a lesson, he assured us, which was often repeated to him and gave him encouragement.

It is well for one who believes in the ultimate prevalence of Christianity to come into China by the way of the Sandwich Islands.

He will receive confirmation to his faith, he will be defended against temptations to unbelief when surrounded as he will be in China with one-half the population of the earth ignorant of the true God, by having seen in the Sandwich Islands what the gospel has done among a race who were as unlikely to be converted as any portion of the human family. If he comes from his ship and steps ashore on the sabbath in China, and sees coopers and blockmakers and boat-builders busily at work, the tailors' shops filled with men plying their needles, the stationers ruling paper, the coolies, instead of horses or mules, carrying every thing, which ever lades a ship, from the quay to the storehouses, the thought will come over him, What progress is the knowledge of the gospel likely to make among this people? Perhaps he spends a sabbath in the country. Here he may look to see the people withdrawn from the requirements which the business of a seaport makes of the inhabitants; but in the country he will find the people as busy with their handicraft or trade as the people of the city, giving no sign that the idea of the sabbath and of the God of the sabbath has visited their minds. He will be overwhelmed with the contemplation of four hundred millions of human beings utterly destitute of the knowledge of God. He remembers how at home his heart used to glow on hearing accounts of additions to native churches, and the rehearsal was followed by joyful missionary hymns sung impromptu, —

> "Yes, we trust the day is breaking;
> Joyful times are near at hand;"

and he asks himself whether he is losing his confidence in the ultimate triumph of Christianity, and in the sufficiency of divine power to turn the hearts of nations, as the rivers of waters are turned. If he be a firm believer in the Bible, he will say, that, while he remembers the conquest of Canaan, especially its first great achievement, the capture of Jericho, his faith never can falter. Were not the aborigines of Canaan devoted to destruction by the Almighty, and their land apportioned to the tribes, with minute directions how to take possession of it, the very line of march prescribed, the great tribe of Judah in the forefront? And did not our Lord spring out of Judah? Has he not upon his vesture and upon his thigh a name written, — King of kings and Lord of lords? While, on returning to his Christian ordinances at home a Christian traveller in China may be less excited than he used to be there at the report of a few conversions among the heathen, because he will have an enlarged idea of the gross darkness which covers the people, he will only have exchanged his former confidence in man for a more entire confidence in God. The accumulation of difficulties in the way of the gospel he will regard only as those barrels of water which were poured on

Elijah's altar, serving to make the fire from heaven more triumphant.

Going into a monastery in China with a clergyman who could converse in Chinese, we saw among the inmates a woman who seemed to be ever praying as she sat a little retired from the rest. The superior told us that she was praying all the time, being overheard frequently in the night upon her bed in supplication. He said that there was some great burden upon her mind which she would not disclose. She was evidently not insane; and, from all that I could learn about her, I came to the conclusion that she was under conviction of sin; sinfulness, rather than any particular transgression, was the burden upon her heart. That there are many throughout the heathen world thus exercised, we cannot question; the second chapter of Romans speaks of them, among others, "with the work of the law written in their hearts." They may be few compared with the whole heathen world; yet how interesting to think that such may be in a state of mind fitting them to accept the gospel, should it be made known to them, and that they will not perish merely for not being acquainted with it. Thus, where sin abounds, grace may much more abound, choosing its subjects independently of human instructors. "Thou canst not tell whither it goeth,"—this superhuman agency. This thought is some little relief to one as he wanders about in those regions of the shadow of death, impressed by much that he sees with the reflection how true to the letter is the apostle's description, in the first chapter of Romans, of the heathen world.

The party of young friends who called on the bride also called at the house of an aristocratic Chinese family, with whom one of their number was acquainted. There were several young daughters and sons in the family, who all spoke some words of English. A missionary's daughter acted as interpreter. The Chinese young ladies brought out their state dresses, which were heavily embroidered with silver and gold. They put them on their visitors, made them walk about the courtyard, following them with shouts of laughter. They then gave them cake and cups of clear tea. One lady belonging to the family smoked a long pipe, and offered another pipe, with opium, to her guests. The Chinese young ladies showed their little feet, apparently with much pride, to the visitors: three inches and a half each was the measure of nearly all the feet.

In a school for girls taught by a missionary lady, the visitors saw pupils from five to fifteen years. The feet of these children were generally swathed, and the girls showed, by their faces, great pain. Mothers came in to listen while the teacher was talking to the children. The girls, when reciting, stood with their backs to the teacher, a mark of respect. They sang several of our familiar sabbath-school hymns.

The steamer from Shanghai to Hong Kong put in at Amoy to bring the cargo of a disabled bark to Hong Kong. This gave some of my family who had been making a visit to Shanghai an opportunity to see Amoy. It is situated on a barren, hilly island; its streets are as narrow as lanes. Going through them in chairs, you come out upon a hilly district, with few trees, covered with remarkable rocks, many of them bowlders, not settled so far in the ground as most rocks, but lifted from it, some of them on their smallest ends, and some leaning toward each other, making natural rooms, with mossy floors, and an opening at the top. Some of them are used as temples on a small scale; idols, discolored by age and damp, are perched in them. Some real temples are built of the largest bowlders. In one of them, as one of the party was sitting on the stool in front of the idol, looking at the hideous images with which the temple was filled, expressing her wonder that human beings prayed to such things, one of the missionaries present asked an old priest if they really did believe in them. He said he could not tell whether the people did believe in them or not. The images might, or they might not, be gods; but "it was the custom to worship them; and, after all, whether they heard or not, it amounted to about the same thing as the worship by Christians of their God."

The foreigners, merchants, missionaries, and others, do not, as a general thing, live in the city, but on a small island across the harbor, rocky, like the larger island where the city is built, but not quite so dreary and barren. Attempts have been made to fertilize it, not wholly without success. Many of the houses are attractive, commanding a good sea-view.

From a great cave called the "Tiger's Mouth," formed by two rocks projecting from the side of a hill, a flat one forming the lower jaw, or the floor of the cave, and the upper stone curving over it, making a good resemblance to an animal's mouth, you look down upon a wild, barren tract of country, where the rocks, my informant said, reminded her of almonds stuck into the top of a Christmas pudding, or as if giants had been having a battle, and their missiles had been left on the field in the reckless position where they fell. One rock, about eighty tons in weight, was balanced on another larger rock so evenly that one man, putting forth all his strength, could make it tilt slightly. They say that a typhoon makes it rock perceptibly. Just below it is a small Chinese cottage. The woman who occupied it was asked if she was not afraid to live there, for if the bowlder should tilt a little too much, one end of it would go through her roof. But she said, "No, it is 'Fung Shuy,' and will bring good luck to my dwelling."

This leads me to speak of "Fung Shuy." Though the literal meaning of "Fung Shuy" is "wind and water," this does not give any idea of the thing.

The Chinese regard the south as the source of good influence, inasmuch as vegetable life, with all the genial influences of spring and summer, are from that region. The north, they perceive, is the source of death to the vegetable kingdom. As animals partake of the diverse influences proceeding from these two opposite regions, they infer that men are susceptible to the same. They suppose, therefore, that there is a vital influence moving all the time from south to north. This may be obstructed. To secure its full effect, they prefer to have their dwellings front south; for they hold that from the north evil influences are constantly proceeding. Even the dead, they believe, are susceptible to these adverse influences. If graves are placed so as to meet good influences, it is called good Fung Shuy. It is a subject of great study to ascertain the influences which promote good Fung Shuy and hinder the bad. Any thing — as a hill, rock, trees — standing due north, and not very remote, especially if the region toward the south is unobstructed, and particularly if water is in that direction, is good Fung Shuy. There are men who may be called professors of Fung Shuy, who are experts in the science. The woman in Amoy thought that the bowlder near her house was good Fung Shuy. The term may be defined, The science of positions favoring good, and shielding from bad, influences. This is related to the extensive subject of ancestral worship, which would lead me too far from my narrative.

One who had for several years been learning the Cantonese dialect gave me some account of it, of which the following is a part: —

There are eight tones, — four high, and four low:

HIGH. 1. Ascending. 2. Circumflex. 3. Departing. 4. Depressed.

LOW. 1. The voice suddenly drops. 2. Low circumflex. 3. Low departing. 4. Falling.

Example, JESUS is pronounced *Yea-so*. *Yea* has the first low tone; *so* the first high.

To show the difference in the meanings of words, according to their pronunciation, take the following: —

   Mai [circumflex], is, To buy.
   Mai [low], is, Do not.

Wan [circumflex], is, To trouble.
Wan [low], is To hunt.

"Pidgin-English" is a singular form of speech which the Chinese language assumes when the natives are first attempting to use English. *Pidgin* means *business*. You are made by it to think of the dialect which we fall into in talking to infants. If any one can explain why infants are supposed to understand us better when we make our words terminate in *ee* or *y*, he may proceed and explain the natural philosophy of Pidgin-English. In talking to a Chinaman you find yourself, as it were, addressing an infantile capacity, imitating his own Pidgin way of speaking, even in talking to an adult. I will give one or two specimens of Pidgin-English, which I found in print. The first is Norval's Narrative, taken, as the reader hardly needs to be informed, from Rev. Dr. Home's tragedy of "Douglas."

NORVAL'S NARRATIVE.

My name is Norval. On the Grampian hills
My father feeds his flock, a frugal swain,
Whose constant cares were to increase his store
And keep his only son, myself, at home.
For I had heard of battles, and I longed
To follow to the field some warlike lord.
And Heaven soon granted what my sire denied.
This moon which rose last night, round as my shield,
Had not yet filled her horns, when by her light
A band of fierce barbarians from the hills
Rushed like a torrent down upon the vale
Sweeping our flocks and herds. The shepherds fled
For safety and for succor. I alone
With bended bow and quiver full of arrows
Hovered about the enemy, and marked
The road he took, then hasted to my friends,
Whom, with a troop of fifty chosen men,
I met advancing. The pursuit I led
Till we o'ertook the spoil-encumbered foe.

PIDGIN-ENGLISH OF NORVAL'S NARRATIVE.

My name belong[1] Norval. Topside that Grampian hill
My father makee pay[2] chow chow[3] he sheep.
He smallee heartee man; too muchee take care that dolla, gallo.
So fashion he wanchee keep my:[4] counta one piecie chilo,[5] stop he own side.
My no wanchee. Wanchee long that largee mandoli.[6]
Little teem,[7] Joss pay my what thing my father no likee pay.[8]
That moon last nightee get up loune, alla same my hat;
No go up full, no got square; that plenty piecie man,[9]
That lobbel man,[10] too muchee qui-si,[11] alla same that tiger,
Chop chop come down that hillee, catchee that sheep long that cow.
That man custom take care, too muchee quick lun way.
My one piecie owne spic eye,[12] see that ladlone man what side he walkee.
Hi-yah! No good chancie findee catchee my flen.[13]
Too piecie loon choon lun catchee that lobbel man;[14] he
No can walkee welly quick; he pocket too much full up.

---

[1] Common word for "is." [2,3] Pastures. [4] Me. [5] Considering I am his only child. [6] That great Mandarin. [7] In a little time. [8] Providence (Joss) provides what my father would not. [9] That band. [10] Robber. [11] Very fierce; chop chop:—quick. [12] My eye alone watched that robber. [13] Could not rally any friends. [14] Two of us soon caught up with him.

We fought and conquered. Ere a sword was drawn,
An arrow from my bow had pierced their chief,
Who wore that day the arms which now I wear.
Returning home in triumph, I disdained
The shepherd's slothful life ; and having heard
That our good king had summoned his bold peers
To lead their warriors to the Carron side,
I left my father's house, and took with me
A chosen servant to conduct my steps,
Yon trembling coward, who forsook his master.
Journeying with this intent, I passed these towers,
And, Heaven-directed, came this day to do
The happy deed that gilds my humble name.

The following is a better specimen, there being fewer liberties in the rendering: —

EXCELSIOR.

The shades of night were falling fast,
As through an Alpine village passed
A youth, who bore, mid snow and ice,
A banner with the strange device,
   Excelsior !

So fashion knockee he largee.¹⁵ He head man no got shottee far ¹⁶
My knockee he head. Hi-yah! My number one stlong.¹⁷
Catchee he jacket, long he trouse, galo.¹⁸ You like look see?
My go puttee on just now. My go home, largie heart just now.
My no likee take care that sheep. So fashion my hear you go fightee this side,¹⁹
My takee one servant, come you country, come helpie you.
He heart all same cow; too muchee fear; lun away;
Masquie!²⁰ Joss take care pay my come your house.²¹

---

¹⁵ We beat him, largely. ¹⁶ Before he had time to shoot. ¹⁷ I am very strong. ¹⁸ Took his clothes; (galo: an exclamation.) ¹⁹ I hear you have war. ²⁰ "Never mind," a Portuguese exclamation. ²¹ Providence led my way hither. — N. B. The Chinese do not pronounce the letter r; for "run," they say "lun."

TOPSIDE GALAH.

That nightee teem¹ he come chop, chop,²
One young man walkee, no can stop.
Colo masquie,³ icee masquie,
He got flag chop b'long welly culio see;⁴
    Topside Galah.

---

¹ ² That night-time drew on fast. ³ No matter for the cold. ⁴ He had a flag which was very curious.

His brow was sad; his eye beneath
Flashed like a falchion from its sheath;
And like a silver clarion rung
The accents of that unknown tongue.
   Excelsior!

In happy homes he saw the light
Of household fires gleam warm and bright;
Above, the spectral glaciers shone,
And from his lips escaped a groan,
   Excelsior!

"Try not the pass!" the old man said;
"Dark lowers the tempest overhead;
The roaring torrent is deep and wide!"
And loud that clarion voice replied,
   Excelsior!

"Oh, stay!" the maiden said, "and rest
Thy weary head upon this breast!"
A tear stood in his bright blue eye;
But still he answered, with a sigh,
   Excelsior!

He too muchee solly;[5] one piecie[6] eye
Lookee sharp so fashion, alla same mi;[7]
He talkee largee, talkee stlong,[8]
Too muchee culio,[9] alla same gong.
    Topside Galah.

Inside any housee he can see light;
Any piecie loom[10] got fire all light?
He look see plenty ice more high,
Inside he mouf he plenty cly;[11]
    Topside Galah.

"No can walkee!" ole man speakee he;[12]
"Bimeby lain[13] come; no can see;
Hab got water, welly wide!"
Masquie! mi[14] must go topside;
    Topside Galah.

"Man-man!"[15] one galo[16] talkee he;
"What for you go topside? look see."
"Nother teem," he makee plenty cly.[17]
Masquie; alla teem he walkee plenty high.[18]
    Topside Galah.

---

[5] Sorry. [6] Each of his eyes. [7] The same as "mine." [8] Strong. [9] Very curious. [10] Every room. [11] Cry. [12] Old man said to him. [13] Rain. [14] I. [15] Stop. [16] A girl said to him. [17] He earnestly answered. [18] All the time he kept on walking.

"Beware the pine-tree's withered branch!
Beware the awful avalanche!"
This was the peasant's last Good-night;
A voice replied, far up the height,
          Excelsior!

At break of day, as heavenward
The pious monks of Saint Bernard
Uttered the oft-repeated prayer,
A voice cried through the startled air,
          Excelsior!

A traveller, by the faithful hound,
Half buried in the snow was found,
Still grasping in his hand of ice
That banner with the strange device,
          Excelsior!

There in the twilight cold and gray,
Lifeless, but beautiful, he lay;
And from the sky, serene and far,
A voice fell like a falling star,
          Excelsior!

"Take care that spilum tlee,[19] young man!
"Take care that icee!" he no man man;[20]
That coolie chin chin[21] he good night;
He talkee, "Mi can go all night."
        Topside Galah.

Joss pidgin[22] man chop chop begin,[23]
Morning teem that Joss chin chin;[24]
No see any man; he plenty fear,
Cause some man talkee,[25] he can hear.
        Topside Galah.

Young man makee die;[26] one largee dog see;
Too muchee bobbery findee he,[27]
Hand too muchee colo;[28] inside can stop,
Alla same piecee flag, got culio chop,[29] [30]
        Topside Galah.

---

[19] Withered tree. [20] He would not stop. [21] That peasant bid him goodnight. [22] The religious man. [23] Soon. [24] Religious address. [25] He heard a voice. [26] Had to meet death. [27] With difficulty found him. [28] Very cold. [29] The same flag with its curious device. [30] Chop is brand, stamp, quality; e.g. first chop.

The mysteries of human speech are impressively illustrated in the ease with which the children of foreign extraction, brought up from infancy in China, learn and skilfully use all these tones and the other niceties of the language. An ear accustomed to music, of course, is a great help in learning this language; but, when a person is in the least dull of hearing, it is not easy to distinguish between some of the words. One thought impressed me in thinking of the language as a barrier against the rest of the world: If the Chinese nature is naturally upright, and if sin is owing wholly to contamination by intercourse with depraved people, how happens it that China does not present us with a people of saints? having been kept by their language, as they have been, from mixing with men. That language has done more than their great wall in separating them from the rest of mankind.

We had a typhoon at Hong Kong, Sept. 29.

I was spending a fortnight at the house of Dr. Legge. On sabbath evening, at sundown, there was an appearance of rain, with some unusual disturbances in the air; and soon the servants came into the parlor with planks and joists to strengthen the windows, the same precaution being used outside. The wind rapidly increased, till the strength of our gale of Sept. 8, 1869, had but a faint resemblance to it. Instead of one blast, there are lulls; then a renewed tempest, increasing in strength while the typhoon lasts, which in this case continued from sundown on Sunday till Tuesday at daybreak. Hundreds of lives were lost in Hong Kong Harbor. The ships were almost invisible from the shore, the spoon-drift being nearly equal to a thick fog. We were grateful that the typhoon did not find us at sea. We could understand the answers of old sea-captains, who on some one in our hearing saying that he should like to witness a typhoon, shook their heads, looked grave, and said, "You will never wish to see another."

Another excursion — by favor of the Messrs. Heard, and of Captain Arthur H. Clark of the steamer "Suwo Nada," plying between Hong Kong and Singapore — was made to Singapore. On the way, we stopped at Saigon, a French port in Cochin China, from which the French were then compelling the Prussians to retire. Rice is largely exported from this place, and opium is received to an amount which tells a fearful story. Here we saw noble specimens of tigers, which are declared by authors of high repute to have devoured, on an average, one man a day through the year, not many years ago, in some parts of the East Indies. They swim over to the islands from the main lands. They approach their victim from behind, felling him with a blow upon the head.

Singapore is about five days by steamer from Hong Kong, including the visit to Saigon. At Singapore you feel that you are in the East Indies, from the luxuriant foliage, the birds of marvellous plumage, the plants such as you never fancied, the groves of cocoa-nuts yielding a supply exceeding belief. The common saying there is, that the cocoanut serves ninety-nine purposes. The rough husk, by being subjected to a powerful pressure, is at once reduced to a fibrous state, ready to be worked into coir mats, or spun into cheap rope. The natural bend of the husk adapting it to the human head, it is carefully prepared and dyed, then worn.

A principal road runs close by the sea, is well shaded, and abounds in delicious odors from the gardens. The house and grounds of a rich Chinaman, Mr. Whampoa, are visited by foreigners as objects of interest. Rare East-India plants, ponds filled with the pink lotus, vines trained or trimmed in fantastic shapes, — such as eagles, deer, lions, and many others, — on frames, trees with great variety of foliage, make the place attractive. A six-legged turtle, which we examined, was an object of much interest to its owner. He is a venerable man, speaks English well, gives free admission to visitors introduced by any one with whom he is acquainted.

It made us feel that we were indeed in Eastern regions to be contiguous, as we were one day, to the residence of a Rajah, the name savoring of Oriental life.

V.

MANILA. — HOMEWARD BOUND.

My country, sir, is not a single spot
Of such a mould, or fixed to such a clime;
No! 'tis the social circle of my friends,
The loved community in which I'm linked,
And in whose welfare all my wishes centre.
MILLER'S *Mahomet*.

Whose heart hath ne'er within him burned
As home his footsteps he hath turned
From wandering on a foreign strand?
W. SCOTT: *Lay of the Last Minstrel*.

There blend the ties that strengthen
  Our hearts in hours of grief,
The silver links that lengthen
  Joy's visits when most brief.
Then dost thou sigh for pleasure?
  Oh! do not widely roam,
But seek that hidden treasure
  At home, dear home!
BERNARD BARTON.

ON the 22d of November we left Hong Kong for Manila, our agents concluding to wait no longer for hemp to fall, but to load the ship with sugar. We took in three million pounds, — enough, we were told, to supply our whole country one day.

We reached Manila Bay Dec. 1, but would not have wondered had we been weeks, instead of five days, in contest with the current and head winds. One day we tacked fourteen times off Manila. At length we dropped anchor in the spacious roadstead, and waited for the health officers and the custom-house officials to inspect us. No one is allowed to have any communication with a vessel until she is officially visited. Steam-tugs would be an advantage to weary mariners contending against the current in sight of anchorage.

We were the guests of a gentleman and his wife, — he a member of the house of Messrs. Peele, Hubbell, & Co. We were there seven weeks, and, even if delicacy permitted, language would fail in the attempt to express what we enjoyed in that beautiful house. Situated at one end of the city in the parish of Santa Ana, we were removed from the noise and tumult of business. The river runs near the house with a current of at least four miles an hour. Immense plantain-leaves stood round, looking like the blades of huge oars; the banana hung in large clusters; the garden was filled with many things to delight the eye. The house covered a large space. You enter it by a spacious driveway, roofed over within the main building. Stone steps lead up to the story on which are all the rooms in the house, high and wide, opening into the large hall. Instead of carpets, floors here are polished, by rubbing them with the plantain-leaf. The house was cool and in all respects most comfortable. The eye is refreshed by constant verdure, the grass in December and January having the brilliant green which our early grass presents in the month of June. It seemed strange to be riding in open carriages at Christmas-time and January, with ladies in muslin dresses, or requiring only light shawls. The atmosphere is clear, and the stars have so peculiar a lustre as to be the subject of remark by foreigners. The river runs about fifteen miles to a lake, by cocoanut groves, and in some places by steep cliffs nearly two hundred and fifty feet on each side, covered with foliage, and having small cascades. In the river there are as many as twenty-eight rapids. Some of our party ascended them in canoes, spending two days on an excursion with a company. One evening a party of gentlemen took a small steamer, the private property of a friend, and went with us up to the lake. It was a moonlight night: the East-Indian scenery, the curves in the steam, and at last the scenery of the lake, made the excursion enchanting.

The society in Manila, composed of American, English, Scotch, and Spanish people, was delightful. Their hospitalities, entertainments, and numberless courtesies make deep impressions upon a visitor. There are no unpleasant distinctions among them; they maintain an agreeable freedom in their intercourse. Indeed, one cannot spend a few weeks in Manila without feeling glad if it happens to be at the close of a long tour; for, as it will be most likely to be pronounced the climax of his social experience, it will be appropriate to have it at the close.

We were near the old Church of Santa Ana, whose bells many times a day remind the faithful of their devotions. They were played skilfully, with a loud noise. At six o'clock in the afternoon, the native inhabitants pause wherever they may happen to be at the vesper bell, and perform their devotions. I frequently met the Archbishop and his secretary in an evening walk, who would stop suddenly when the bell struck, and, uncovering their heads, repeat their prayers. I visited most of the churches. Imposture nowhere reigns with more open demands upon the credulity of the people. In one of the churches there are large paintings of the "Holy Girdle," whose marvellous cures, and power over serpents, and the bestowment of blessings in answer to faith in it, are described in large letters for the people to read. Each of the many parishes has a monthly procession, in which the population join. One evening we encountered a procession which blocked the street for two hours. Four thousand women, in black, filled each side of the wide street, chanting Scripture and prayers, the men occupying the middle of the street with an imposing show of images of canonized people surrounded with lighted chandeliers. Each woman in this procession had a lighted wax candle which she had bought of the priests, to be returned to them after the march. This is the source of a large revenue to the Church. These processions keep up a lively enthusiasm among the people.

The manufacture of the Pina articles employs the people at home. These articles, such as veils, handkerchiefs, &c., are made of the fibre of the pine-apple; at almost every house in some of the poorer parts of the city you see this work on small frames, exposed to the sun. The men are very many of them occupied in the training of game-cocks; frequently every tenth man you meet will have one of these birds under his arm. One sabbath we were told there was a fight between a tiger and a buffalo on exhibition. The buffaloes are meek, docile animals, used instead of oxen. Their horns are wide-spread and very long. The buffalo took the tiger on his horns, threw him high, and the fall indisposed him for further effort. Some of the most beautiful objects here are the trees filled with fireflies. Sometimes, all along a road, the trees will be crowned with the small creatures, their light constantly emitted; so that the tree looks as though it were filled with gems. Few sights are more attractive. The inhabitants resort in the evening to the Pier, which is a solid structure extending a sixteenth of a mile into the bay, a sea-view on all sides; and once a week there is music by the bands, which draws crowds. Much of this Spanish music is more sentimental than we are accustomed to hear addressed to the populace, exciting a thoughtful attention.

Manila is the capital of Luzon, one of the principal of the Philippine Islands. The climate in December and January was intensely hot. After nine o'clock in the morning, it was not agreeable to be out of doors, even to drive; but at five in the afternoon, and in the evening, the cool sea-breezes made it pleasant to be abroad. Religious services are sustained on sabbath evenings by a few Christian friends at the house of one of their number, but there is no public place of Protestant worship there. It was instructive to go from China, from the depths of heathen idolatry, into the depths of formalism, under the name of Christianity. You question whether you have advanced at all into the light of truth; for, though it is a relief to be where the Scriptures and the names and forms of Christianity are heard and seen, you are impressed with the bias of the human heart to idolatry. To come from heathenism in China, and Roman-Catholic superstition in Manila, into Christian temples here at home, makes you wonder that only a certain number of leagues of salt water separate between such places as Canton or Manila, and Boston, both in the same world.

ANJER.

We began our homeward voyage from Manila Jan. 20, and reached Anjer Feb. 1. Anjer is the eastern point of Java; vessels pass it to and from the China seas. "Passed Anjer," in the marine reports, signifies that a vessel has left the China seas on her homeward way, or has just entered them on her outward voyage. Anjer supplies vessels with poultry, vegetables, fruits, and water. On inquiring for bananas, we were told by a man who came on board that he would get us "a fathom of them for a dollar." It was a large Oriental statement, with a basis of truth.

Batavia is about seventy-five miles from Anjer; the road to it is characterized by Dutch solidity and thoroughness. Opposite the hotel at Anjer is a banian-tree said to be the largest in diameter in that part of the world, composed of shoots which have descended from the top, taken root, and become principal parts of the tree. We saw from shore our ship under sail beating about against a head wind and current. The sight was animating. We rowed off to her four miles, glad to be on board the noble thing which had borne us more than half round the world, and was waiting to complete the great circuit. As often as we now see in the marine record, "Passed Anjer," we recall the sensations with which we looked off from that lighthouse, which is the first or last object of interest to all who navigate those East-Indian seas.

CAPE OF GOOD HOPE.

It was extremely interesting to be approaching this famous point. That great maritime revelation, the opening of a new route to India in 1487, the story of Bartholomew Diaz and Vasco da Gama, and of the first navigators around that point, who used to bury their journals and set up a stone pointing to them, that the homeward-bound vessels might, by this primitive mail arrangement, get the latest news of them, made it an object of deep interest. Here the astronomers come from afar to observe the signs of the heavens; and certainly no place can be conceived of more favorable for such purposes. The clear atmosphere and the perfect horizon make it a place well fitted for telescopes to try their power. The Indian Ocean, opening here, spreads before the observer the scene of some of the most interesting events of history. Being about four thousand miles from north to south, and of equal breadth, and receiving the Red Sea, holding the Persian Gulf and the Bay of Bengal, distinguished by such islands as Madagascar, Mauritius, Ceylon, and by such rivers as the Tigris, Euphrates, Indus, Ganges, and by the great equatorial current, which, after it leaves the wide coast of China, crosses this ocean to the Mozambique Channel, seeking the east coast of Africa, and making its way by the Cape of Good Hope, — this Indian Ocean does not yield in historic or natural interest to the two greater oceans. Its northern part, divided from the southern by the Tropic of Capricorn, floats the commerce of Europe and this country with China, India, and the Malay Islands. Arabia and Persia, and the opposite India, have used its waters for centuries in their local commerce. Points of interest along its seacoast, gulfs, and rivers are Aden and Mocha in Arabia, Bassorah in Turkey, Bombay, Madras, Calcutta, in Hindostan, and Point de Galle in Ceylon. It seemed more like the centre of the world on this ocean than elsewhere. Its astronomical attractions and its sunsets give it a peculiar charm.

Table Mountain, which makes the most

TABLE MOUNTAIN AT CAPE OF GOOD HOPE.—page 125.

prominent object at the Cape of Good Hope, though not the southernmost point, is 3,816 feet high. It has a flat summit of great extent, and from that peculiarity in its formation it has its name. It is seen in clear weather fifty or sixty miles distant. You would think it a burial-place of kings, having something stately in appearance, as though it were a mausoleum erected by human art, a work like the pyramids, built by successive generations. We sailed away from it in the latter part of an afternoon, reflecting that we had looked upon the last object connected with the continents of the other hemisphere.

ST. HELENA.

We came very near this deeply interesting spot, which for several years held the attention of the world. We could appreciate the saying of the notable prisoner there, who spoke of himself as "chained to this rock;" for the island impresses you as a huge rock.

Very few isolated places seem to have more connection with the world; for twenty-five vessels on an average each day pass by it, showing their signals, to be reported. To begin and speak of the place, and the thoughts and feelings which it suggested, would not be expected. We could not go ashore without first entering the ship and paying port duties; but we had a full view of "Longwood," where Napoleon lived, and where he met death.

We resolved to go on board a British man-of-war which we should pass not far off. On lowering the largest boat into the water, the seams proved to have opened, and she soon filled. The gig which we used all summer in going ashore at Hong Kong was more seaworthy; so we set off in her for the man-of-war. We took four men to row and one to bail, which he had to do nimbly, the water gaining on him, obliging the stroke-oar to lend him a hand. By keeping our feet on a level with the rail, we managed to reach the

"Rattlesnake" without being wet, though we discussed the question whether a handkerchief at half-mast on an oar would be likely to be seen if we were swamped. We went and returned safely, having received from the ship the news of the French and Prussian war, three months old, and having also received of a New Bedford whaler some vegetables, which we tried to pay for in vain.

The last point on which our eyes rested was the Island of Ascension, always interesting to every one at school as the most solitary-looking spot in the dreary South Atlantic. A whaler tacked and came near us; two of the men stood aloft watching for whales. Feeling that they were the last of our race whom we should behold for some time, and with sincere respect for the hardy men on their ocean hunting-ground, I waved my hat to them, and the two caps aloft made hearty response.

We soon found by the signs above us that we were entering the northern hemisphere.

One evening we saw, just above the horizon, two stars of "The Dipper." It was several nights before the North Star came up the watery hill. The poet Spenser probably had never sailed in these latitudes when he wrote of the North Star as never being below the horizon : —

> "By this, the Northern wagoner had set
> His sevenfold teme behind the stedfast starre
> That was in ocean waves yet never wet,
> But firme is fixt, and sendeth light from farre
> To all that on the wide deepe wandering arre."*

But at last it came up, dripping wet, and inspired in us the hope of soon watching it from our windows at home.

HOMEWARD BOUND.

While it is true that as much was combined as could be wished for to render this voyage agreeable, those who have been at sea will not believe that we were free from the ordinary discomforts or annoyances of sea-life.

---

* The Faery Queene, B. 10, c. 2. 1.

For the satisfaction of those who have suffered in sailing-vessels, it will be well for me to show the dark side of sea-life in some of its principal annoyances; doing this, however, for the sake of the truth, that the voyage may not appear to have been out of the ordinary experience of those who go down to the sea.

One of the first things which we all suffer at sea is revealed in the inspired account of sea-faring experience, which we are presented with in the contrasted experience of being on shore : " Then are they glad because they be quiet." There are times at sea when stability seems to be the most enviable state. In weariness, the invalid passenger, tossed and not comforted, feels constrained to quote one of the earliest verses of inspiration : " Let the dry land appear." Yet there is so much that provokes mirth in the midst of discomfort, that it is not easy to say on which side the balance lies, — whether of discomfort or amusement. Behold three men, two of them, at least, used to the sea, setting out from different parts of the main cabin to make their way to the table in the forward cabin. The ship rolls over on her port side, and the cabin-floor is at once an inclined plane at a grade very much removed from horizontal. They have a steep hill to ascend; and a seven-pound weight on either foot, ashore, would not be more cumbrous than that which seems now to be holding them to the floor. The sensation in trying to move cannot be unlike that which would be felt in an exhausted receiver. If the weight of the atmosphere on the human body, fifteen pounds to the square inch, instead of being equally diffused, could be concentrated on the feet, the sensation probably would not be unlike that which one feels in trying to get across a ship's deck when she is thrown over to the side opposite to that whither you are going. So these three gentlemen stand immovably fixed in the middle of the floor, their feet discreetly wide apart to preserve the upright position of the body. Then the ship rolls over on the other side, and the three travellers to the dinner-table go involuntarily fast to the side of the cabin, and hold on by a door, while the ship rolls once more, and comes back, it may be, with mitigated severity. At last a favorable opportunity is seized, and the three slide into their seats in postures more necessary than graceful. Then begins a series of mishaps at table. No careful adjustment of the dishes, nor even the security provided for them by the racks, can guard against the accidents which befall cups and saucers, indiscreetly filled, or plates of soup not well provided with suitable dunnage of slices of bread underneath the lee side. A barrel of apples falls against the door of a locker and empties itself over the floor; and a canister of lamp-oil, whose cork had not been made tight, follows after the apples, and they are no longer eatable. Oh, to be quiet! What seems more desirable than a good foundation?

One day, when the ship was rolling heavily, it was difficult to keep your seat on the settee, and impossible to lie reclined. Every thing which was not lashed to some fixture about the room, or to staples driven into the floor, was sure to adopt a nomadic state, and go from side to side. Among other things, a "Pilgrim's Progress," which had been left on a table, fell from it and went sliding to and fro, exciting lively sensations in me at the thought that Mr. Ready-to-Halt and his daughter, Much-Afraid, were moving at a pace ill suited to the crutches of the old gentleman; for the book went like a shuttle back and forth on the floor.

The little stove in the cabin felt the changeable wind, and did not draw well. This required the frequent attention of the steward. He was a colored man. He sat on the canvas carpet whittling, to make light-wood to start the fire. The ship went down on one side, and the steward with it, whittling all the while, then sliding back in his upright position maintained with becoming gravity, till the passengers, no longer able to contain themselves, were made merry at the sight. This made him show his white teeth, silently, without any thing so undignified as a laugh; at which the passengers were increasingly merry.

What shall I say of the cockroaches, red ants, tarantulas, and mice? One thing can be said in favor of all of them, — they were not mosquitoes. This was a nightly consolation; but it was the only good thing which could be said of them all. The ants would cover every vessel in which they could find any thing to drink; fresh water seemed to be their chief delight; if a sponge wet with it were hung up to dry, on taking it down, the little creatures would be there in legions. The white ant is the bane of the Indian climate; their depredations, however, are chiefly on shore. I was going up the front stairs of a gentleman's dwelling in China, when his foot went through a stair. "Ah," said he, " the ants have been at work here!" But at sea we found the cockroaches most destructive. It is not pleasant to find several of them on your pillow when you go into your stateroom at night. They are harmless to the person, but the covers of books, and every thing which had been pasted or glued, all lacker work, and paper generally, suffer from them. Yet there are housekeepers on shore who can inveigh against vermin, as well as people at sea.

There are some people who cannot bear any noise overhead at night. If the gale does not wake them and keep them awake, twenty or thirty sailors, hoisting or lowering the spanker, their boots making a noise not unlike that of horses in a burning stable, will do it. If the stillness of the night and the passenger's sleep are broken by the mate pacing the deck to keep himself awake, the heels of his boots will be chiefly answerable; for these make the principal disturbance; he cannot comfortably wear India rubbers during his watch; he is to be pitied if he has a nervous passenger, and thanked if he is able to forego his walks for the invalid's sake.

It would seem as though there should be a special punishment for those who practise fraud in ships' stores. Your appetite is delicate; you have no source of supply but your locker; that is furnished with bottles and jars which profess to hold, for instance, jellies, made and provided expressly for sea-faring appetites. Your hopes of a comfortable supper are vested in a jar of jelly, which the steward has placed on table, hoping to provoke an appetite. On opening it, instead of the fruit jelly, which the label assures you is within, you find only gelatine, flavored with an extract resembling the fruit. There is nothing on the table for which you feel any desire but the promised jelly; you find yourself secretly invoking a sea-faring experience like this upon the man who has so deceived you, till at last your suffering is so great under your disappointment, which grows intense as the tasteless supper proceeds, that in sheer self-defence against this provoking ship-chandler you feel compelled to forgive him, promising him, that, if you ever go to sea again, you will pay special attention and see if his name is on the labels of the jellies. He who writes this and they who read it will not fail to remember that invalids are apt to be querulous and unreasonable. So small a matter as a jar of preserves disappointing the expectation of a nervous patient, especially at sea, where there are no means of alleviation, may be more than a match for the philosophy and even religion of the best of men and women.

When I have said these things, very few discomforts or annoyances remain which are not incident to almost any situation on shore. Many things there we are freed from at sea: the noise of cats at night, the barking of dogs, the scream of locomotives, the painfully regular puffing of stationary engines, the roar of wheels, the annoyances of mischievous boys, — these you escape at sea;

all of them in sailing-vessels, for in steamers you have some of them. If one should fairly add up the comparative discomforts of ship and shore, would life at sea prove to have the most of them? I came to the conclusion that a good sailing-ship, with agreeable company, is as near a perfect state of rest and peace as ever falls to our lot.

"Tarring down," as the vessel is coming near to port, is to a landsman an animating sight. Every rope in the standing rigging, beginning aloft, feels the smearing process, which is carried on without gloves. The stays which run between the masts at an angle of forty-five degrees are reached at every point by the boys, each in what is called a boatswain's chair, not unlike the seat of a swing, in which he is lowered at his call by a boy or the mate on deck, who belays him at each descent of a few feet at a time. Often have I watched these boys, suspended a hundred feet above the deck, wiping the rope with the sopping rags, which they dip in the tar-bucket, till they reach the deck; and I have thought what a sight one of these boys would be to his mother, — her pet, besmeared with tar from head to foot, one suit of his clothes kept for the occasion doomed to go overboard, as tarring down is reserved till near port; the boy feeling an honest pride as he illustrates in his work the dignity of labor. But perhaps the mother's heart would yearn toward her child more than when she should see him in " the boatswain's chair," on seeing him at his meals. He has no table. He goes to the galley with his tin pot; the cook gives him his portion of tea or coffee, sweetened with molasses; the boy cuts a piece of beef from out the mess-kid, gets a piece of " hard-tack " from the " bread barge," sits down on deck, or on a spare spar, lays his tin pan beside him, and, with his sheath-knife and fingers, despatches his " grub." Many, with their feet under rich mahogany tables loaded with China-ware and silver, would give it all for the boy's appetite and power of digestion.

If there were hours when we might have been made afraid, it was not in gales nor in the raging of the sea; but in some peaceful, moonlight night, when every thing was beautiful to the eye, we saw that we might have reason to tremble. If the insidious current should take the ship and prevent her from passing a certain headland, we might be stranded on a desolate coast, and see the ship piled up, a helpless thing, in the sands, and ourselves left to the horrors of want. We would be passing a forlorn place in the China seas, for example, and the current might prove more than the wind could overcome; we might be swept round a point where we heard the surf roar on the beach, and it might depend on a favorable change of wind in a few moments whether we should drift into deep water and go round another point, or whether that spot was to be the graveyard of our noble vessel. At such moments, life re-appears to you with its long-forgotten passages, and the future seems filled with pictures of woe such, perhaps, as you had never seen even in dreams. At times like these you have experience of the special care of God, are made to feel the practical value of the doctrine of a particular providence, you receive instruction in the nature of prayer, learn more lessons in faith than years of ordinary experience can furnish, more convictions of the privilege and duty of childlike confidence in the Almighty, such that you are persuaded a thousand temptations to unbelief cannot overcome. There are paradoxes in one's feelings in times of imminent danger. It is easy at these moments, strange as it may seem, to forget your own possible loss and sorrow, and lose yourself in thinking of your ship, of which you may have felt so proud, and which, having borne you half round the globe, must, perhaps, now bury her stem or stern ignobly in the sand, all her rich panelwork being made of no account by the waves breaking ruthlessly in through the rent sides, the spars and sails left free to be the sport of the tempest, and soon her freight melting away in the surge. You feel that you would sacrifice any thing short of life itself to prevent such disaster. And when suddenly the wind comes round the headland, and you find that you have met a favorable breeze, and the ship goes safely again on her way, you wonder at yourself, perhaps, for rejoicing in her deliverance equally with your own.

The rudder affords a constant fund of interest when the ship is at her full speed. The parting and closing water makes incessant forms of beauty; you may hang over the counter and look down into the wake for a long time, and not be weary. The swift rush of the water to close up the furrow made by the keel keeps attention awake; the graceful sinking of the stern in alternation with the bows, bringing you down, now to a level with the waves, then far below them, brings apprehension enough with it to make a novice question why he has never heard people who have seen it describe their pleasure. When night has set in, and the phosphorescence happens to be abundant, kaleidoscopes never revealed such wonders to the eye. Sometimes you will be startled by a flood of luminous matter going past the ship. It is called "whale feed," supposed to be an accumulation of animalculæ which Nature has provided for the sustenance of some of her offspring in the deep. "These wait all upon thee, that thou mayest give them their meat in due season. That thou givest them they gather."

We had religious services every sabbath morning, when the weather allowed, at nine o'clock. Almost all hands would attend, it being left optional with them. On the way from the Sandwich Islands to China, in the trade-wind region, we had the service on deck. No preacher ever enjoyed the sight which met his eye in the objects around his pulpit more than those which were seen from that place of worship. Immediately around the speaker were twenty-five sailors, well dressed, wakeful, well behaved; an awning was over them; their singing was animating; the beauty of the ocean scenery, the sight of distant vessels, the sound of the water as the ship went through it, contributed to the enjoyment of the sabbath stillness, which seemed to have at sea, as on land, a hush unlike the week-days. While natural scenery cannot inspire the heart with spiritual emotions, yet, when these exist, they are sometimes assisted in their peaceful and their elevating power over us by a contemplation of such a prospect as we had on that deck in those sabbath hours. We had three different crews in our long voyage, making in all about seventy men and boys who sailed with us. The most of these placed themselves under religious influences while on board: now they are scattered like the gulf-weed which went by us; but, in the different vessels in which they now sail, they may feel the power of some good impressions which they received; for not only on the sabbath, but in the weekly Bible-class, they were affectionately exhorted by their captain, who added to his spiritual efforts for them kind instruction in morals, useful information on subjects relating to their calling, and to the younger portion of them lessons in navigation and practical seamanship. Several libraries had been presented to the ship. We had one boatswain who was a singer. He would spend a large part of an evening frequently in his room on his chest, with his feet on his bunk, a pipe in his mouth, a small hymn and tune book in his hand, from which he would sing almost all the hymns set to lively tunes, pausing occasionally to keep the pipe from going out, then beginning again, perhaps with the words, "Oh, how I love Jesus!" "Say, brothers, will you meet us?" the sailors sometimes making respectful intimations to him that they would like to sleep. Some of them will be likely to remember words of his hymns. But most of the sailors showed by contrast the value of early education in furnishing the mind with religious ideas as well as the letter of scriptural knowledge. It is doubtful whether "George Andrews," at his time of life, can succeed in solving that great mystery " how an 'elephant' can go through the eye of a needle;" though, had he begun in youth, he might have received instruction which would have at least reduced the elephant to a camel. Some sailors, like him, awaken affection for them which it is pleasant to cherish. But the sea-birds are hardly more vagrant now than they.

May 16, at 11, A.M., we took a pilot off New York, and at 9, P.M., dropped anchor, having been gone nearly nineteen months, and, including our excursions from Hong Kong, having sailed forty-two thousand miles. All this time no sickness, accident, loss, nor painful delay had occurred. Our only regret was that the voyage had come to an end.

In looking back upon it and recalling pleasurable seasons, those which most readily recur to me are morning hours on deck alone with a Bible. I only repeat the experience of every one who loves the Word of God. The mind, freed from care, sees in the Bible at such times meanings which grammars and lexicons never can impart. Nature might reveal things most wonderful at such a place as Singapore; but, in a psalm read in the silence of the sea, there would often appear marvellous things in the language of Scripture, in its simple incidents, in the characters portrayed or acting themselves out unconsciously in their trials and joys, which would create an interest never excited by the plumage of East-India birds, or coral branches, or curiously twisted and beautifully enamelled shells, or by the marvellous light on insects and creeping things, or by precious stones, and pearls, and fine linen, and purple, and silk, and scarlet, and all thyine-wood, and cinnamon, and odors, and ointments, and frankincense. I cannot forget the impressions made upon me by reading connectedly all the experiences and the language of the prophet Jeremiah. They were like the strange constellations which rise to view in low latitudes. I have felt among the wonderful things of God the truth of that inspired declaration, "Thou hast magnified thy word above all thy name."

On reaching home, it was deeply interesting to find, at sick-beds, in stricken households, and in circles where the goodness of God had filled pious hearts with thankfulness, that one need not travel to be filled with all the fulness of God. "Neither is it beyond the sea, that thou shouldest say, Who shall go over the sea for us and bring it to us, that we may hear it and do it?" I found that some who had not left home for two years, but had toiled in shops, and counting-rooms, and laboratories, and domestic life, had been increased with the increase of God.

IT IS EASIER TO GO ROUND THE WORLD THAN THROUGH IT. But in going through it we are tempted to think, perhaps, that in solitude, with its retirement, we can have more of God's presence than in the busy scenes of life. This led me, at the close of our voyage, going back with restored health to busy scenes, to resolve that I would endeavor to guard against the feeling that there are places or conditions to which God's presence is confined. Not in the solitudes of ocean, nor in rural scenes, "neither in this mountain nor yet at Jerusalem," need we be, to enjoy communion with God. The thought I embodied at sea in these lines: —

PRIVATE WORSHIP IN THE CAMP OF ISRAEL.

  My God, how good to be
  In the wilderness with thee
When Israel's tribes pursued their desert way.
  Leaving the Red Sea strand
  To find the Promised Land,
Thou shepherdedst thy flock by night and day.
  So great a change in that one night!
Pharaoh no more, the God of gods was then their risen light.

  Treading the deep sea floor,
  Dry shod from shore to shore,

The wall of waters piled on either hand,
    Hearing the rushing waves
    Fill up the Egyptians' graves,
The foremost vainly struggling for the land.
    Thee would I love with all my soul,
My heart should rove no more; God should possess the whole.

    Encamped where Elim spread
    Her palm-trees overhead,
With wells of water springing all around,
    Not the new-found fruit
    Would so my longings suit,
Nor the cold water from the pebbly ground
    Could so revive my spirit there,
As when in some still place I sought my God in prayer.

    Now moves the ransomed host
    Far from the sea-washed coast,
And plunges deep where foot hath seldom trod;
    And see that cloud by day
    Marking out their way,
Guiding them safe as by a royal road.
    My God, I could not see that sign,
And not with rapture cry, My soul, this God is thine!

    And when the night came on,
    The fading twilight gone,

Or whether storms or stars should fill the sphere,
 That pillared cloud grew bright
 With more than earthly light;
No need of words to whisper, God is here.
 Finding some place beneath the sky,
My God, my very present God, nightly I'd cry.

 When manna strews the ground,
 And quails the camp surround,
And when the rock breaks forth in living streams,
 And cities walled to heaven
 To them were freely given,
Wonders of grace, exceeding all their dreams,
 My God, each day and hour I'd be,
With heart and soul, a living sacrifice to thee.

 To see the words in stone
 Graven by God alone,
To hear the voice which from the darkness spoke,
 To see the man of God
 Trail his princely rod,
And cry, "Forbear! my soul doth fear and quake."
 Oh, could I ever sin again!
Would not my soul become thy living temple then?

 Behold the priest-borne ark
 Resting in Jordan; mark!

It tarries till the host are all passed o'er,
    Then slowly leaves the stream;
    The friendly waters seem
Listing till every foot has reached the shore.
    How sweet to live, how safe to die,
That wondrous ark of God before me passing by!

    But pause, my soul! and see
    If Israel's God to thee
Hath not approached in loving-kindness nigher;
    What place like Bethlehem!
    The Saviour's footprints deem
Steps leading up to God, ascending higher.
    Hast thou forgot Gethsemane?
The world's four thousand years had not a Calvary.

    How hast thou loved and prayed?
    How feared, adored, obeyed?
Is God in Christ less than a pillared cloud?
    Are words he wrote in stone
    More than the Word, his Son?
Is not "the living way" the better road?
    Surely, whate'er thine eyes can see
In Israel's favored lot, falls far this side of thee.

    Awake! awake! my powers,
    And Israel's God and ours

Love, serve, and worship with a double flame;
   God's ancient methods learn;
   The elder Scripture turn,
Tracing therein the great Immanuel's name.
   So shall thy worship perfect be,
And both the Testaments shall shine full orbed o'er thee.

www.ingramcontent.com/pod-product-compliance
Lightning Source LLC
Chambersburg PA
CBHW030316170426
43202CB00009B/1024